George Sharland

Knapsack Notes of Gen. Sherman's Grand Campaign through the Empire State of the South

George Sharland

Knapsack Notes of Gen. Sherman's Grand Campaign through the Empire State of the South

ISBN/EAN: 9783337173616

Printed in Europe, USA, Canada, Australia, Japan

Cover: Foto ©ninafisch / pixelio.de

More available books at **www.hansebooks.com**

KNAPSACK NOTES

OF

GEN. SHERMAN'S GRAND CAMPAIGN

THROUGH THE EMPIRE STATE OF THE SOUTH,

By GEORGE SHARLAND,

PRIVATE CO. B, 64TH REG'T ILL. V. V. INFANTRY, 1ST BRIGADE, 1ST DIVISION, 17TH ARMY CORPS.

——— ———

RESPECTFULLY DEDICATED TO THE GALLANT ARMY OF THE TENNESSEE.

———

SPRINGFIELD, ILL.
JOHNSON & BRADFORD, PRINTERS.
1865.

PREFACE.

To THE READER:

It is at the urgent and repeated request of numerous members of the company and regiment, of which I am a member, that I have finally concluded to venture the hastily penned notes that compose this brief sketch on the wave of public criticism, and in so doing, I am fully aware of its inadequacy to meet the various wants of many into whose hands it may possibly fall; but when it is understood as being my first attempt at publicity, and that they were originally written with a simple view to gratify my own desire to preserve some of the grand links of that mysterious chain of events that has characterized our country during its passage through the most fiery ordeal, and through one of the most terrible commotions that ever marked the history of any nation, I trust it will lead to the exercise of that leniency necessary to the encouragement of an early effort, and that which always marks the course of a liberal and magnanimous public.

It is published principally for circulation in the division and corps to which I belong, and it is necessary to state in this connection that I have invariably aimed at, and endeavored in my statements, to underrate rather than overrate matters and difficulties as they occurred during our line of march through the state; but my statements and observations are principally based on the stand-point of view that I occupied in the regiment, brigade and division to which I am attached, and in consequence I could not do that justice that I earnestly desire to do to all engaged in this daring and noble sacrifice. I have avoided, as much as was possible, giving undue prominence to any particular regiment or brigade, as I consider all equally worthy of credit, and entitled to the respect of a generous and confiding public. The hours of commencement of each day's march, and the time of encampment, together with the various particulars connected with the division during our forty days raid, may be said to be strictly a true reflection of raiding life (as far as it goes) throughout our entire army, as the same scenes and occurrences are alike presented in every division and corps. But there are a "thousand and one" things connected with our romantic movements and operations by the wayside that I should have noticed more at large had I previously anticipated its preparation for the press, and which time will not now admit of on account of pushing forward its publication before the final disbandment of the army.

It has been written, for the most part, under all conceivable and exciting circumstances, and in every possible attitude, for want of better accommodations, and having invariably shouldered the musket as a private in the ranks, subject to all the caprices attendant on active service and raiding life, I trust that the candid reader will overlook any defects that may present themselves in its perusal consequent upon its hurried publication.

GEORGE SHARLAND.

KNAPSACK NOTES

OF

GEN. SHERMAN'S GRAND CAMPAIGN.

CHAPTER I.

FROM KENESAW MOUNTAIN TO ATLANTA.

The Situation and Review—The Midnight Destruction of the Railroad and its Appearance—The Link of Communication Severed—Real Condition of Affairs—Comic Scenes—Arguments by the Wayside—Crossing the River—Our Second Arrival at Atlanta—The Grand Preparation—Loading the Trains—Final Visits to the City and its Results—The General Appearance and Final Arrangements—The Destruction of the City—Its Sad Reminiscences—Terrible Fruits of Treason—Order of March—The Backward Look and its Suggestions—The Solemn Funeral of the City—The Closing View—The Duties of Provost Guard—Playing Opossum—Red Tape—Sad Wayside Scenes—Night Marching—Interesting Views for the Artist—Cruel Results of War—The Cause of our Slow Progress.

November 12th, 1864, finds us at Ruff's Station, situated between Marietta and the Chattaoochee river. At this camp we arrived on the eve of the 5th, weary, footsore, and worn out from hard marching and excessive fatigue, from a forced march of thirty-two days pursuit of the rebel Gen. Hood and his forces, having successfully accomplished the object of the trip. Here, then, having rested about six days in order to prepare for a more important campaign, and the troops having been amply clothed, as a judicious and necessary precaution, we, early on the morning of the 12th, were, with the whole division, ordered out on review by Maj. Gen. Mower, commanding the same, and, in military parlance, a sure indication of something yet in store and soon to be developed by the bone and sinew of the army, like the prophet's cloud of the size of a man's hand, that continued to expand until the horizon was darkened by its gloomy shroud.

Scarcely had the review been accomplished when orders were issued to break camp, and in a brief space of time the plain just now so thickly dotted with the whitened tents of our brave boys now assumes its wonted appearance, and ere fifteen minutes has elapsed the vast area so thickly peopled with the veterans of many a battle-field is deserted, and they are seen in well arranged columns on the highway, with polished guns and bristling bayonets gleaming in the sunshine, many conjectures passing from one to the other as to their probable destination. A few hours suffice to develop the object of our trip, for after a heated march of nearly nine miles we are brought to a stand on the line of railroad on the north side of the

Big Kenesaw Mountain soon to figure in history. Stacking arms, we commenced the destruction of the railroad, vigorously prosecuting the same until midnight, the long line of fires, with its curling wreaths of smoke, giving evidence how well we had accomplished our object. Having performed our task, we bivouacked for the night, each taking shelter as best he could from the inclemency of a cold and piercing wind.

Nov. 13th: At 3 A. M., ere some had scarcely got asleep, the regiment was aroused from its slumbers and ordered hastily to fall into line, as we had to reach camp left yesterday by 7 A. M. It being extremely cold, the effects of a piercing wind, the joke was not well relished by the boys, who felt much like an old bachelor when prematurely aroused from an after dinner nap, and, as a result, imprecations would be sometimes called down on the heads of those who were the cause, especially when, in their hurried steps, they would stumble over rocks and stumps in rounding the Kenesaw. In the course of a few hours fast marching, about 7½ A. M., we brought up in camp left yesterday. Unburdening ourselves of all the essentials of a soldier's kitchen, larder, wardrobe and the all-important weapons—emblems of our invincible law and calling—and the forty rounds of rebel hard tack, we proceeded to hurriedly cook our breakfast and demolish the same, as only soldiers can when their appetites have been whetted pretty keenly by a previous march of seven or eight miles. Having masticated our usual amount of hard tack, and eased it down, the way of all the earth, by a quart or more of steaming beverage we call coffee, the assembly sounded, and packing up our invincible cargo and decorating our persons with the same, we fell in line of march, and bidding a long farewell to the place of our recent sojourn, we pulled out on the road for Atlanta.

No sooner were we fairly under way than conjectures were fairly rife among the boys, as they are at all times when in the execution of a new move, or the commencement of a new campaign, as to our probable destination and the result to be accomplished thereby; and amusing as are the decisions of some in reference to the next most important position to be gained, others display such acuteness in their chain of logical acumen that many commanders might profit by their plain and convincing arguments. As we are bustling along the road thoughts arrest the attention of some as to the real condition of affairs. Having severed the link of communication that connected us with the north, they look back to see the effects of yesterday and last night's work, and as the buildings and piles of railroad ties send up alternately their volumes of flame and smoke, making the atmosphere murky with its presence, expressions, varied in their nature and meaning, escape their lips, and finally to solve the mystery of the scene in the wide-spread surrounding desolation, with an approving nod, exclaim: "The just fruits of treason and rebellion!" But suddenly some scene of a comic nature turns up, and the whole line reverberates with the echoes of a hearty yell, the evidence that something good has been relished by them. Thus alternately reason and amusement find room for exercise as we pursue our onward course. And here let me remark that there are but few questions of present or future policy that concern the interest of our country but what are overhauled and made to pass in scathing review in their arguments with each other, but for the present they consider the all absorbing attention of the nation should be the speedy suppression and overthrow of this causeless rebellion, and thus they suffer much to accomplish the same, making their actions speak louder than their words.

Having traveled several miles in this way, we suddenly stumble upon our, and the rebel works, north of the Chatahoochie, which changes the general subject of conversation, as they view the various contrivances resorted to for the better warding off of those ripping bullets, intended as so many messengers of death. When rounding the bluff at this important point, we are brought in full view of the river near Jenning's ford, where our army crosses the river for the third time; first, in the advance on Atlanta; second, in pursuit of General Hood; and, lastly to penetrate the centre of the rebel confederacy. Having crossed the river, we rapidly pushed on our way until nearly dark, when we brought up, and went into camp about two and a half miles south of Atlanta, midway between the same and East Point, having marched since three A. M., from the north side of the Rig Kenesaw, a distance of thirty-one miles, stopping only for breakfast in the meantime. Having secured our necessary fuel, it being very cold, we prepared our suppers, and doing ample justice to the same, we erected our "dog tents" and turned in to snooze for the night, forgetting all our troubles, as we calmly resigned ourselves into the arms of Morpheus.

Nov. 14th: At five A. M. we were aroused from our slumber by the sound of reveille, in the numerous regiments composing the Army of the Tennessee. It was not long before all was life and bustle throughout the entire camp, only one day being allowed thoroughly to prepare for our departure on the morrow. All the division trains started for the city early in the morning, each to take in their apportionment of rations for the campaign. More clothing was also issued to those needing them. Numbers of officers and privates visited the doomed city for the last time, previous to departure, many of them returning at night in high glee, having used a liberal quantity of what the Indians call "wild-fire," while others of their comrades, more unfortunate than themselves, enjoyed the luxury of a few hours rest under guard, till the fiery potion had well nigh ceased to operate on their combative organs, and feeling pretty flat from the effects of a previously over-excited imagination, they could be seen wending their way to camp in the various directions of their respective regiments; and, we trust, a little wiser if not better by the adventure. Thus the day passed, and it was not until late in the night that the noise of revelry and mirth were hushed to silence, and all retired to their respective tents, leaving nothing but the camp fires with their slowly burning embers as evidence of the conviviality that previously existed.

Nov. 15th: This being the day appointed to bid a final adieu to the Gate City; and knowing the length of time it takes a large army to straighten itself in proper line of march, were not permitted to enjoy an overdose of sleep, and as early as 4 A. M., a conglomeration of music was heard in every direction of our immense army, and where darkness previously existed, a thousand brilliant lights could be seen looming up beautifully bright, forming a contrast with the surrounding desolation, like so many stars issuing from the shroud of a dakening storm cloud. All parts of the camp exhibited signs of thrift and bustle. This is an important day to the army commanded by the brave and gallant Sherman. This is the last day for those who are to join our army from the north to do so, or they will be left amid the gloomy desolation. For several days, preparations have been making in the city, for its overthrow. The Gate City, which a few short months since was filled with rebel troops, and whose streets were teeming with thousands of helpless citizens, the heart of the Confederacy, whose pulsations beat high with confederate

hope, through whose iron channels troops and munitions of war were constantly
passing and repassing, whose shops and foundries were unceasingly moulding the
missiles of destruction, over whose head tons and tons of molten lead and iron were
being hurled for the space of forty-six days, as so many harbingers of its fate,
where the sound of mirth and the drapery of mourning could be heard and seen in,
direful contrast, that city with its miles of encircling works, offensive and defen-
sive, and its massive forts, whose suburbs furnished graves for thousands, both of
loyal and disloyal victims of this most sanguinary struggle, the city that had long
fed the Confederate army with the fruits of its treason, from the numerous outlets
for many months; that city to whose inhabitants the sound of artillery and musketry
had become gravely familiar for many a day; that city made classic by the bloody
conflict on the extreme left flank on that memorable day of July 22d, when that
brave and gallant hero, General McPherson, fell mortally wounded, as also the conflict of July 28th on the extreme right, and other signal engagements during its
important siege; that city with its splendid depot, and other important buildings,
and its machine shops, evidence of the years of former industry and wealth, "whose
clustering merchants raised the busy hum, and planned the schemes of commerce,"
is soon to feel still the withering blights, and the scourge of war, the sorry fruits
of rebellion and treason.   The lesson of destruction is soon to be signally displayed.
Already can be heard in the distance the thunder of explosion; the ministers of its
wrath are hurrying on the work of its destruction.   Destruction it dealt for many a
day, and now it is reaping the result and double measure is dealt out in all its
stern reality.   The public avenues that led to the highways, and brought in the de-
velopment of its resources, were previously closed; the iron horse no longer gives
forth its accustomed signal; a death like silence already pervades the public and
private workshops; the merry chiming of bells no longer evinces the happiness and
prosperity of its inmates.   Desolation already sits enthroned within its precincts,
but the final retribution it has invited, is reserved till now, when preparing to take
our final farewell.   But to return.   At break of day the assembly sounded its preparation to depart, and regiments could be seen rapidly forming, and taking up their
line of march for another field of operations.

The acres of tents which had just now overspread the surface, like the sails of a
ship when a storm threatens, are hurriedly reefed, and assigned to the knapsack.
The long lines of muskets in well arranged stacks, that just now stood in harmless
silence on the color line, can now be seen gracefully reclining on the shoulders of
the brave who know how to wield them, and now assume a more threatening aspect.
The immense square of wagon trains that a short time since were motionless, can
be distinctly seen forming gradually into a long line of march.   Orderlies, swiftly
riding and passing each other at every angle, could be seen passing and repassing
as the bearers of dispatches to each commander in the different camps.   All are
sufficiently apprised of the order of the day, and cast your eyes where you will, all
is bustle and activity, as there is no time to be lost; and gradually each army corps
takes up the line of march assigned it by the prime mover and commander of an
army thoroughly inured to the hardships and difficulties of active service—the order of march being thus: The 14th army corps occupies the extreme left; to its
right is established the line of the 20th corps, and next in order is the 17th army
corps; while on the extreme right, can be seen the 15th army corps, with its su-
perb fighting material.   Each corps has its own line of march separate and distinct,

while all act in combination to secure the same end. Fairly under way, many an eye is turned to look back toward the city whose destruction is inevitably secured. Explosion after explosion has been heard during the hours it has taken to form and disappear, each in their respective lines of march, but the backward look, as it views the dense volumes of smoke, ascending up as so much incense to atone for the crime it involved itself in, in time past, is not the look of sympathy or pity, but rather the loak of approving justice in the measure of atonement required; for the last three and a half years of hard service with all its wearisome marches, its numerous conflicts, and incessant exposure to the inclemency of alternate heat and cold, and the various diseases incident to camp life, has enstamped upon the brow the indelible work of stern justice, and now as they look, their lips inaudibly express the justice of the measure. Not that they admire the infliction of the stroke, but like a merciful, yet stern judge, they think it necessary for the honor of the law, and as a measure best calculated to shorten the heated contest of civil strife. And yet further, the vigorous siege with all its bloody scenes and associations is yet fresh in their memories. The conflicts of the 20th, 22d, and 28th of July, is not yet erased from their minds, for here brothers, uncles, cousins, nephews, father and son, and sons and fathers, were mournfully separated from each other; old and valued friendships and acquaintainces were rent in twain, ne'er to match themselves again with the wily and treacherous foe on the gory battle-field. The tedious days and nights spent in the water-soaked trenches under the constant crackling of musketry and the hoarse and savage shrieks of those iron monsters, as they belched forth from a hundred cannon, loomed up fresh in their minds; the many victims of deliberate aim on the skirmish line are not forgotten; the numerous tons of iron and leaden hail that issued from its centre and sent so many thousands of our brave comrades to an untimely grave during the summer months, brings up the sad reminisences connected with it.

The day is cloudy, the sun refuses to shine, the sky has clothed itself with its drapery of mourning, habiliments well befitting the solemn occasion. No longer the Gate City, throbbing with high life, but an isolated center, fit emblem of the widowhood that is to follow. Its suburban shades, soaked with the blood of our brave, and now containing the moldering remains of their lifeless forms, call to high Heaven to be summarily avenged, and their cries are heard. The destroying angel is abroad, and while the work of destruction is being executed, and the vast sheets of flame purify the atmosphere tainted with the blood of the innocent, the darkening clouds veil the solemn sight from the bright and blue sky, and like so many pall bearers, kindly attend the solemn funeral and purification of the city, and shut in the sorrowful scene from the outer world, and now and then shed its tears over the scene in the form of light sprinkling showers, for be it remembered that while it is solemn work, and the act of retributive justice, yet it excites compassion in the mind of many a brave, as they recede from the solemn view, but consider it expedient for an example and warning, and as a necessary sacrifice, " That the whole Nation perish not."

Thus matters stand. As in the distance we recede from the sorrowful view, leaving the remnants of the city shrouded in its fatal gloom, to do penance and keep Sabbath until the day of its resurrection comes round.

To-day our division, it being the 1st division of the 17th army corps, is assigned to the rear of the corps, our brigade rear brigade, our regiment rear of brigade,

—2

and our company to the left of the regiment, having been assigned to the duty of rear and provost guard, whose province it is to pick up all stragglers from their respective commands, unless provided with proper documents to show that they are so authorized. This sometimes proves a disagreeable task, for, in the case of a large army like ours, it must be that some, from accident, sickness or otherwise, will be found far in the rear of their respective commands; in consequence, our duty necessitates us to urge them on faster than their physical strength will oft-times permit them, although provision is made for such cases in the supply of divi-ison ambulance trains attached to each division; but in order to secure transportation in the same they need a passport from the regimental surgeon, which cannot always be secured by the unfortunate applicant, for various reasons, some of which I will try to enumerate. In the first place it seems to be taken for granted by regimental surgeons and others that every regiment contains certain members who design, to play the opossum, or in common military phrase, "to play off on the surgeon" for a sick man, when in reality they are sound and healthy. Thus confusion often ensues in the exercise of the judgment in the case of the would-be patient. Second— It is ofttimes the case that a soldier really sick makes application, stating fully his case, but from an apparent healthy looking countenance is refused the privilege; while another, with a more pallid and bleached appearance, is admitted, although more than a match in physical strength and endurance for the other. Third—It is of no use to cloak the fact but that red tape, or favoritism, finds a free and easy channel to manifest itself in, in military as well as in civil and political life, so that some can always secure the requisite documents, while others, really sick, expe-rience the cold shoulder to their fervent appeals, and often exhausting all their energy and strength in the prosecution of their journey, drop down by the wayside in utter helplessness. I will adduce the necessary proof in support of my assertion, and appeal to the Army of the Tennessee for its verity, that is, when we hur-riedly moved out from East Point, in pursuit of the rebel Gen. Hood. They will remember seeing the sickening sight of many of our brave comrades left dead by the roadside for want of needed help. It is a black spot on our military horizon, and at its remembrance many sad and gloomy pictures intrude on our memories, and soften our affections, somewhat bronzed, by the oft-repeated scenes in our military experience. But they are not all such cases that we meet with straggling in the rear, but rather some refractory ones, who feel very huffy and insolent at being compelled to walk under guard, and plainly indicate their disapprobation of such treatment, but philosophically conclude that a caged bird that can walk and won't walk, in military tactics, is made to walk, they reluctantly conclude it best to follow. And thus, during the day, we are continually adding recruits to our num-ber, and some from a class generally found in that particular province. Reaching camp we turn our trust over to the provost marshal, who examines into the nature of their several cases, rendering his decision and disposing of their several cases in accordance therewith.

Having, we trust, sufficiently explained the duty of rear and provost guard we will return to the march. About 1 P. M. our whole army left Atlanta in the rear, and our attention is now thoroughly turned to the coast. The advance is already in camp, or nearly so, but the difficulties connected with the progress of a large train are great, and owing to the same, the rear has not made many miles of pro-gress. And while we are slowly wending our way along our course, being south-east, the general conclusion among the boys is, that our destination is Savannah. For when once the line of direction is marked out by the course we are steering, the boys generally decide pretty correctly the rallying point to be gained, just as the pointers of the dipper, or great bear, invariably point to the polar star. For when, on the 25th of May, we withdrew from the siege of Atlanta on our last grand flank movement that preceded the capture of Atlanta. Ere we had reached the West Point & Montgomery Railroad the decision had been generally rendered to this effect, that the possession of the only line of railroad south of Atlanta left the rebels was the object to be gained by the important move, and the same was fully realized. Other proofs could be adduced to show that their judgment in such matters often proves correct. Darkness comes on apace and the general appearance of the horizon indicates a disagreeable night, and as the progress of the train is impeded and brought to a stand, we turn into an open field on our left and hastily prepare our coffee. After supper, the train being motionless, we gathered around our several fires and began to review and talk over the incidents of the past, the conversation being interspersed with hearty jokes, and merry laughter on the part of the listeners, until the way was cleared for our further advance—fifteen miles a day being our daily allotted task during the campaign ; and having made but a short distance of our journey, we are necessitated to travel for the night, which often proves very disagreeable, but it must be done, and our progress proving rather too sluggish for comfort, it being rather chilly from previous showers, and the boys always apt to provide for their own comfort as well as circumstances will permit, are seen building fires along on each side of the road, and as the train during the tedious hours of night, only advances by fits and starts, the boys can be seen at every halt, huddling around the fires in groups, varying in their number and oft-times presenting a very interesting scene for the artist's pencil. Now and then, as the clouds disappear, the queen of night, in all her silvery brightness, looks down with queenly pride, as if anxious to ascertain our maneuvers, and then again, recedes from our vision, taking shelter behind her graceful curtains, as if to inform us that it is high time to retire ; but war, cruel war, often knows no night, no day, but is sternly exacting in its demands, insatiate with blood, it is at all times unrelenting in its severity toward the objects of its fury, and knows no settlement until it has been fully appeased in the payment of its stern exactions. But as time passes on, we reach the spot that explains the cause of our slow marching, and passing it, almost equal to "Bunyan's Slough of Despond," we glide more nimbly over the surface, until the dawning rays of twilight announce the Lord of day, as ever ready to dispense its cheering light anew. The mules and horses being thoroughly jaded and hungry, they stop to feed and take a short rest, although four miles in the rear of our advance and camp, while we prepare to cook our breakfast, which consists principally of hard tack and coffee—having traveled only eleven miles during our first day's march from the doomed city.

CHAPTER II.

FROM ATLANTA TO GORDON.

Scarcity of Forage—General Appearance of the Country—Results of Compulsory Labor—Wayside Interrogation—Ludicrous and Comical Exhibition—The Serious Results—Untimely Disturbance from Rest—Difficulties Connected with a Scanty Wardrobe—Approach of the Town—Flight of the Inhabitants—Rush of Swarthy Recruits and their Performances—Series of Dissolving Views—Liberal Appropriation of Forage for Man and Beast—Arrival at Jackson—Hearing the Ocmulgee—Junction of the Two Corps—Return of Foragers—Negro Impressment—Crossing the Ocmulgee—Interesting Race and Its Results—Destruction of Stores, Factory and Mills—Disagreeable Night—Arrival at Monticello—Its pleasing Exterior—Polite Salutations—Destruction of a Gun Factory—Stated Hour of Revielle—Arrival at Hillsboro—Jeff. Davis and His Effigy—The Rush for West—Maneuvres of Troops —Rail Brigades and Divisions the Planters Dread—Various Modes of Cooking and the Variety of Dishes—Unique Sayings and Expressions—The Drenching Storm and Baptism of Water—Salutary Regulations—Gloomy Appearance of Things—Mutiny among the Pack Mules and Steers—Night Marching and the Principal Music of the Occasion—The Rival Contest—Grand Night Scene—Late Arrival in Camp— Troops Caught Napping—Introduction to the Lowlands—A Marked Change—Arrival at Gordon.

Nov. 16th: Having taken our usual refreshment, and the mules and horses enjoyed a short rest, and it being absolutely necessary to make up lost time, we promptly take up our line of march, and being far in the rear the advance division does not, as usual, wait our coming up, and then take the rear, but at its appointed time for departure keeps on its line of march, for it would hinder the general progress of the whole corps to await our arrival. Being accustomed to take matters as they are, the boys kept a stiff upper lip, and coursed on in their usual manner, sometimes fast and then again slow, as the case might be.

The country through which we passed yesterday was very good, and well adapted for farming purposes, but was very barren of everything in the shape of forage for either man or beast, from the fact that everything pretty much had been culled from it for the use of our army during the siege ; and subsequent to the capture of Atlanta, in our quarters about the same. But the appearance of things to-day indicate a greater plenty than is usually found near the outskirts of a large army like ours, so that the horses and mules heartily testified their approbation of its appropriation to the army, in the eagerness with which they devoured it. But being rear guard and having our charge to watch and care for, our time had not yet come to enjoy the common luxuries of the sunny South. For in the main line of march of an army, everything in the line of eatables is taken in out of the wet by those that are in the advance, leaving the rear only the scanty pittance of their refuse, and sometimes not that. But the regulations governing an army in its line of march are wisely ordered for this and other reasons, which I shall hereafter give. The soil and general appearance of the country, if anything, is better than that passed yesterday, and the timber principally oak and pine, the whole well watered by numerous little springs and streams. As we pass along our route, now and then, a large and stately mansion can be seen standing out in bold relief, reminding one of its being the product of compulsory labor and toil, while near by can be seen in more dwindling proportions, the numerous huts, whose swarthy inmates produced the wealth of the lordly proprietor, the whole scene being a sad comment on the injustice of such a course. About noon we were relieved from our charge, and took our place in the ranks of our regiment, and not at all sorry for the change, seeming as though we could walk better, and breathe more free than before. We continued our way until nearly dark, when, having for the past thirty-six hours, with but little change, our knapsacks strapped to our shoulders with all of our indispensables, and no sleep, the general wish and longing desire was for camp. In consequence, every one traveling in an opposite direction, would be interrogated all along the lines as to how far it was to camp; but such is the case that in passing along the lines of several regiments that the same uniform question is asked. The persons interrogated are not always careful to answer correctly from its constant repetition, and thus we have learned not to put implicit confidence in the testimony of transient passers by. However, we have ascertained sufficient to know that several miles has to be made ere we reach our resting place, and in consequence the boys have concluded to nerve themselves for the arduous task. After dark the scenes of the previous night are made to appear, only in a more ludicrous and comical exhibition, for be it understood that it is no easy task to bear the burden of a soldier's fit out for nearly forty-eight hours without rest or sleep, and in consequence as we are occasionally brought to a stand on account of some obstacle in the front, the boys take advantage of the opportunity, and ere many minutes have elapsed, some can be seen supporting themselves against a tree, and by their accompanying nod signify their approval of the same; others huddling in groups around the fire, can be seen making enormous lounges in various directions, ungracefully yielding to the effects of caloric, while others prostrate themselves in the road, seemingly careless of their dangerous position. In fact, Morpheus seems to reign supreme on land as Neptune does on sea, but by the time they begin to dream of luxurious tables loaded with the delicacies of cultivation, and downy beds of ease whereon to repose their aching limbs, they are unceremoniously aroused from their reveries and hurried forward on their line of march; but Morpheus unwilling to loosen the grasp he has on his victims retains them in his hold, until some projecting stump, or root upsets their precious carcase, or on others until some mud hole receives them in its folds. And, whilst it may present an enchanting scene to the eye of the artist, it is anything but agreeable to the suffering victims. But at 2 o'clock in the morning we reach camp, and being weary and worn out, without much ceremony or preparation, we lay down to rest for a few hours, camping within two miles of the town of McDonough, the county seat of Henry county, and about thirty from Atlanta, having traveled about nineteen miles during the day and night. We experienced a few light showers during the day, but the weather was otherwise favorable.

Nov. 17th: In order that our division, which has been in the rear for two days, may take the advance, it is necessary that we should be early on the move. So about 5 A. M. the sound of revielle announces the necessity of an early start. As a natural consequence, it seemed to us severe, and hard to bear, having had only three hours to rest our aching and weary limbs, but the contemplation of an early camp, imparted a new impetus to the remaining strength of the boys. So after considerable effort and rubbing they managed to pry open the organs of vision unusually glued together, as if determined not only to assert, but stubbornly to demand their claims and just rights. Having become sufficiently apprised of the emergency of our case, it does not consume much time to prepare our knapsacks for the day, and cook and devour what little we have to eat, the elements of which are very simple. Our wardrobe and bedding is very scanty, for the most of us travel without a single change of clothes, and a woolen blanket, half of a tent and rubber, with other little requisites, is all we feel able to carry, together with our rations and cooking utensils, &c., &c. The nights being very cold and chilly, during the fall of the year, we scarcely ever enjoy the peivilege of sleep, with our clothes off, as we would suffer much from cold; so that in the morning, or in fact, at any hour in the night, it does not consume much time to place ourselves in a combative attitude. And from commencement of fall until spring, during active campaigns, such as the present, we are necessitated to put up with this great inconvenience, and when an opportunity offers to wash our clothes—which is not very often—we have to put the same hurriedly on, without being properly dried, and when we can wash and boil our clothes without soap, we think ourselves fortunate, as there is none issued on the campaign, and a company camp kettle is almost an unknown luxury in the rank and file.

Having got ready to march, at half past 6 A. M., we broke camp, and our brigade being in advance of division and corps, we pulled rapidly out, and glided nimbly over the surface, as if it was the intention to reach camp at an early hour, or travel a respectable distance, which was fully realized ere darkness set in. We had not traveled far, before we passed the previously named town, most of the inhabitants of which fled at our approach. It contains a court house, and a few other respectable appearing dwellings, but is not very large. The country was well adapted to farming purposes, and very well improved, considering the state of southern society. Our band and martial music, elicited much admiration and surprise among the negroes, numbers of whom could be seen keeping time to the tunes and airs that were played. And look in what direction you please, numbers of them could be seen skulking off from their recent owners to join the Yanks., with their unwieldly bundles of clothes on their heads—a mode of carrying peculiar to the South. Some with their little papooses strapped to their backs in a shawl; some with kettles, others with beds; some laden with the rich plunder of their recent owners, that are now fugitives from home. All of them evincing a clear instinct of self preservation, and come to us fully prepared with everything but eatables, for their exodus from bondage, and their supposed exit from future servitude—thinking shortly to be introduced to the "promised land flowing with milk and honey"—supposing their care and toils nearly ended—forcibly reminding one of the ancient Israelites' exit from Egypt to the Wilderness. But they do not follow the army far, before they have to go through the process of mental investigation, in a thousand and one questions that are put to them by the curious and inquisitive of the ranks. If the reader has been in any of our New York or Philadelphia courts of common law, and witnessed the severe tests to which the witnesses are sometimes put, then is he able to judge of the test to which these sons of Canaan are put, by many of the boys, in their relish for fun and pleasant jokes, at the expense of these swarthy sons of toil. Others, with much alacrity, perform their dancing jigs as evidence of their satisfaction for the new state of things, while some stand by the wayside, politely saluting everything that comes along, that is owned by the Yanks, as they call us, and producing roars of laughter all along the lines by their peculiar manœuvres and curious antics. But our march is pretty rapid to-day, and the whole appearance of things reminded one more particularly of a series of dissolving views, as one scene after another burst upon the vision, as we hurriedly passed along. But shortly before dark, we passed through the town of Jackson, the county seat of Botts county, and went into camp, on the east side of the same, having marched about twenty miles through a very fine country, containing abundance of forage for man and beast, which was liberally appropriated for army use. The rear of corps did not reach camp until late in the night. The day was very warm and close, and roads favorable to travel, making things to have the appearance rather of spring than fall.

Nov. 18th: Our division being in the advance of corps yesterday, it comes our turn again to take the rear of same. But reaching camp the previous night, at a seasonable hour, and leaving the same in the rear of the van this morning, we felt well prepared for our march, having secured sufficient rest the previous night. At 5 A. M., we were aroused from repose by the usual manner of revielle, and at 7 A. M., we strung out on the road, a certain number being apportioned to every wagon as the train passed along—our whole brigade being train guard—whilst our whole company was detailed as foraging party for the regiment. The introduction of the day was warm and pleasant, and continued so until near night, and the roads being good, and country generally undulating, we made rapid progress until we neared the Ocmulgee river, and extensive mills and stores at this point, when the army turned in to a temporary camp, while the pontoons were being laid across the river. The pontoon train traveling wth the 17th army corps, and the 15th corps occupying the extreme right, it is necessary for us to converge and form a junction at every main or principal stream. So laying two bridges, both corps cross at the same time ; and so on the extreme left, the 14th corps forming a junction in like manner with the 20th, thus effectually preventing the weakening of the centre ; and so after each crossing, the extreme right and left branch out again, to their proper place. We brought up about 2 P. M., and it was not long before the foraging parties were returning to the camps from every direction, richly ladened with the delicacies of the South; and it is really amusing to notice the various contrivances resorted to for the means of transportation for the same. Some could be seen with splendid horses, attached to silver mounted carriages and harness, driving in aristocratic style, the results of their adventure; some with light vehicles or buggies, driving like fast young men, with mules attached ; others. not so fortunate as to secure horses or mules, get ropes and thereby attach steers, and even cows to buggies and carts, being the works and style of the olden time. Others still, made pack carriers of the same ; and some, with the ingenuity and perseverance not to be thwarted for want of horses, mules or steers, had fastened on some robust negroes, and on the plea of military necessity, had compelled them, (according to Southern phraseology), to tote their stuff to camp, thereby causing their owners to make some pretty wry and sober faces; in fact, numerous subterfuges are resorted to in various ways, for the transportation of their eatables to the army market, which of course would not exactly stand competition with Washington market, New York, for reasons that I will hereafter give. Yet, nevertheless, answers the purpose very well, under our peculiar circumstances. But there are others that

consider themselves very unfortunate because they have to "tote" the same after
they have secured it. . However, let it suffice that all manage to make their arrival
in camp by night; and all could be seen during the hours of evening, doing ample
justice to the same, in the eager and unceremonious style in which they made way
with it.

About dark we received orders to be ready to move down and cross the river at
a moment's warning.   The third brigade of our division also received orders to
move at the same time, and it being quite an object to secure the first passage
across the river—and both brigades being fully up to the advantage to be gained
thereby—as soon as the bugles sounded for us to fall in, a race was at once commenced.   The third brigade lay in our front nearer the river, which gave them
somewhat the advantage of us; but in order to make that up, our brigade bore off
left oblique, taking it cross lots, and bearing down the bluffs that skirt the margin
of the river at this point, with great rapidity, and came in contact with the advance
regiment of the third brigade, the 10th Illinois infantry, which rather had the advantage and lead of us; but having previously received precautionary orders to
keep well closed up, the advance regiment of our brigade cut the 10th Illlinois in
the centre, and completely flanked them at the Pontoon bridge; but a part of the
10th Illinois regiment having previously crossed, our brigade, on reaching the opposite side of the river, were being repeatedly interrogated as to what regiment, and
not finding the left of their regiment, were completely non-plussed, and could hard-
ly comprehend such an unlooked for occurrence.   In fact, it seemed strange to
them, and they had in consequence to wait for the remainder of their regiment and
brigade, whilst ours pushed on its way to camp.   Jokes were freely and liberally
exchanged between the contestants, as we passed along at the result, and all ended
in good spirit, being looked upon as one of the fortunes or misfortunes of war, in a
noble and manly contest for rivalry and zeal in a good cause.   During the evening
and night, it was very showery, which made it somewhat disagreeable, and it was
dark as pitch, making it very difficult to grope our way along, and slippery in climb-
ing the rugged bluffs, which particularly characterize this romantic district.   Traveling about two miles from the river, we went into camp about 9 P. M., under
strong forebodings of a very disagreeable night, which were fully confirmed—having traveled about twelve miles during the day.   The large cotton factory, with its
immense stores of cotton, and grist mills with large quantities of other stores, were
burned—leaving the factory ladies and other inhabitants of this particular section,
a poor prospect of obtaining a livelihood for the present, until the closing results
of this rebellion brings about a better state of things.

Nov. 19th: Saturday finds us all astir at 4 A. M., although it was a very disagreeable morning, and not pitching tents for the night, our rest was not of the
highest order, and being discommoded by the elements during the night, it was not
a very difficult task to bestir the entire camp to action, and preparing our usual repast, to satisfy the cravings of nature, and drying our blankets, unusually wet with
the watery element, that found us unprepared for its reception, we again packed up
for the "knapsack drill," moving out at 8 o'clock, for our usual race for the coast,
which all anticipated to see ere long.   To-day, our division marched in the centre
of corps, third division in the advance, and fourth division in the rear.   During the
day, we made good time, considering the rain of the previous night, and about the
middle of the afternoon we passed the town of Monticello, situated in Jasper county.

It exhibited signs of unusual good taste and improvement, and looked like Eden in comparison with other places we have passed in the Confederacy. The front yard of nearly every dwelling was tastefully laid out and decorated with evergreens, and flower beds, ingeniously arranged, and filled with the flowery beauties of nature in lavish profusion, whose delightful odors filled the atmosphere with their rich fragrance, and the breath of their delicious perfume ; and had we been transported suddenly from some uncongenial clime, we should have concluded it was the rich products of spring, rather than the mellow ripeness of autumn. The negro domestics of the most wealthy portion of the population came out in large numbers for the purpose, I suppose, of enjoying a good side view of those whom the Masters call, "Blue-bellied Yanks," but they were cleaner and more neatly attired than those usually seen on our journey, and corresponded somewhat with the general appearance of things; and numbers of them could be seen, politely bowing and scraping, as only negroes can, to the rank and file, as they passed along, which must have proved a severe task, before the whole army passed in review. One old negress especially deserves our notice, as she stood in the middle of the street, in front of a large and costly dwelling, where we had to file right. Her constant exclamation was, " God bress you, massa, we're glad you come," and constantly going over the same, while the boys, anxious for sport and fun, would ask her all manner of curious questions, too numerous to mention here, and testing her wits to the utmost to find answers to the same. But one suspicious mark of disloyalty and treason was seen here, in the form of a gun factory, where many a deadly weapon had been manufactured, that perhaps caused the tide. of life's crimson blood to flow from many a loyal heart, struggling to maintain the government at all hazards. It, with its contents, was consigned to the flames, and buried in oblivion's dark hour, and forever made powerless to the rebel foe. Leaving this town, as the fell swoop of war marked it, we coursed on our way five miles south-east of the same, over a good country, where we went into camp for the night, about 5 P. M., and about seventeen miles from the river and mills. We experienced some showers in the morning, but the remainder of the day was very pleasant, and the night very disagreeable and wet. The boys being pretty tired and weary, you may rest assured that camp was a welcome quiet to us, and we accordingly endeavored to make the best of our time in the form of rest, and in the consummation of that which the country afforded us.

Nov. 20th: Sunday morning as early as 4 o'clock—which seems to be the general hour of reveille, throughout General Sherman's Grand Army—we were all in action, as our division had to move out on the road punctually at 6 A. M.; our division being in the advance of corps, our brigade in advance of division, our regiment in advance of brigade, and left in front, so that our company was in the advance of the whole corps. The morning was showery, nevertheless we made considerable headway, and about four miles from the last encampment, we passed the town of Hillsboro, containing a few stores, a number of private dwellings, and one or two churches. But one circumstance I must relate, as witnessed here in passing the town. It seems that some soldier, fond of a joke by the way, had taken a lot of old clothes, which he formed and dressed so as to represent Jefferson Davis, and then suspended them to the rafter or beam of the awning in front of a store, so as to have it conspicuous for all to see it, as they passed by, through the main avenue of this little town. It excited many a pun and joke among the boys, as they

—3

witnessed its exhibition in passing. But leaving the town, we passed on a pretty fair jog during the day, over a more rolling and romantic country than that passed yesterday, crossing some good streams well adapted to milling purposes, and some extensive mill dams built on the same, with grist mills in fair supply. During the afternoon we halted near by quite a large mill. While the pioneers were fixing a foot bridge for the infantry to cross the stream on, the boys taking advantage of the halt, could be seen wending their way down the bluff and across the same, and in a few minutes returning with their haversacks full of meal, and for some time a constant rush could be seen going and coming loaded with the spoils—many of them bearing the appearance of self constituted millers ; for in the pursuit of supplies for the haversack, they allow no common obstacle to arrest their attention, or hinder their progress. At 5 P. M. we reached camp, and the boys having an unusual supply of rations, are congratulating themselves on a hearty repast, and a fine time. To a person unaccustomed to the arrangements of troops in the field, they would be surprised at the active and numerous manœuvres of the troops, in reaching camp. Fancy to yourself a large and wealthy plantation, surrounded and divided off with well constructed fences, for a mile or two in every direction, in the brief space of five minutes, cleared of everything, and present nothing but the appearance of a vast uncultivated plain, and yet such is the fact. For as soon as each regiment ascertains the whereabouts of its color line, two or three from each company can be seen rushing in wild haste in every direction of the camp to the fences, and piling up each for their respective companies ; and as soon as they have stacked arms, each man instantly puts off for his share—all presenting the appearance of rail brigades and divisions. The planters dread to see them more in this aspect of their warfare than any other, as it entirely cuts off their hopes from the prospect of a next year's crop, but such is the dreaded fortunes of war. As soon as fuel is secured, the next race is with kettles and canteens in the pursuit of water, while others start the fire, while some can be seen plucking grass and weeds and running in search of straw, or anything whereon to repose for the night, and this is generally all done in less time than it takes to relate the same. After these things are secured, should any one unaccustomed to the shifts and turns in the army, pass through the different camps, and see the various modes and manner of cooking by the different messes, according to their different ideas of the same, they would acknowledge that it presented a picturesque appearance. And to visitors from the refined walks of life, the various dishes, as they are served up, might not appear very inviting, but to these hardy sons of Mars, they are delicious, and are devoured with much avidity. In raiding life, the dishes are composed of a greater variety than in garrison, as we are necessitated to take the raw material as we find it, and convert it into palatable dishes, as the limits of our cooking utensils, or time and circumstances will permit—our principal supplies consisting of corn meal, sweet potatoes, and fresh pork, with occasionally a little molasses or honey as luxuries. Should the lover of puns, jokes, and unique sayings and expressions, be present during the process of cooking, and the period of its consummation, he would here find a rich feast, and a variety to suit the numerous tastes of individuals ; for here nature shows itself in all its freshness, and presents itself in all its peculiar freaks, for there is no restraint to its generous outflow ; and in consequence, it flows spontaneously from all its inner depths, presenting itself in its genuine homespun, without fear or favor. But this evening, ere some have cooked their suppers, the windows of heaven seem to be opened, and the rain pours down as only it can beneath a Southern sky, compelling the boys to retire within their shelter tents, in order to do justice to their prepared repast. And during the whole night, the rain continues to pour down with unabated vigor, converting the plain into a temporary swamp, sweeping under everything in the shape of shelter, completely saturating the blankets of the boys, making it very uncomfortable for repose, and rendering it almost impossible to sleep. But the thought of stemming the torrents of nature, as well as that of rebellion, on the plea of military necessity, renders them, after some gruff mutterings, to bow in submission to nature's stroke.

The third division of our corps being in the rear, did not reach camp until morning, the roads being so excessively miry, causing slow progress to the train, depriving the boys of rest, and exposed them to the severe storms of the night.

Nov. 21st: After a good night's soaking, one would think that we ought to be well limbered up for another day's advance, but such is not exactly the case, and in turning out from our watery recess, the first thought and action predominant in the mind, is to secure a good fire and dry our clothes and blankets, that feel unreasonably heavy from its recent baptism of water.

It was at break of day when we issued from our hiding places. The rain was still continuing to pour down in all its fury, as if determined to check our advance; and hastily and unceremoniously making way with our morning meal under disagreeable circumstances, we attempted to steam out the subtle contents that had taken shelter in our dry goods, or rather wet, as best we could. But the fourth division taking the advance, and occupying some time to string out in line of march on the road; and our regiment having to take the extreme rear of our division as rear train guard—we did not move out from camp until 11 o'clock in the morning. I would here state, as promised in a previous chapter, that the salutary regulations governing an army in its line of march, are wisely ordered for various reasons.

1st. In the line of march of a corps, it is necessary that each division should take its turn in the front, for the roads getting so badly cut up by the advance trains, that it would soon kill the horses and mules in the rear to keep up; and the same effect would work its way also on troops, as the rear would enjoy but little sleep, on account of not reaching camp until midnight, and sometimes not at all; consequently the division in the front to-day, takes the rear to-morrow, and gradually works up again in its proper turn. The same order is also maintained in brigades as well as divisions, and in regiments we march alternately right, and then left in front, thus giving all parts of the rank and file an equal change.

2d. Were the regulations not maintained, the advance division of the corps, would secure daily an unequal share of the forage, while the rear would be scantily supplied, and this is quite an object, where a large army like ours depends principally on the country for supplies.

3d. It is also necessary, in case of meeting with much opposition from the foe, and in the capture of horses and mules to supply the places of those worn out, and various other reasons will suggest themselves to the reader, that I have not time to enumerate here. But there is another feature in our line of march consequent upon such campaigns as the present, and that is, to give the trains the full benefit of the road, while the army proper, marches through the plantations on either the right or left side of the road, thus gaining a threefold advantage. 1st. Expediting the progress of the train. 2d. Forming a strong guard to the same. 3d. Thwarting the effects of a sudden cavalry dash, which might otherwise occur; and being cut off from communication, it is necessary to preserve the rations, as we know not what awaits us at the coast.

Nature and the appearance of things look gloomy this morning, but still the army is not entirely without its enjoyments; for while the boys are pulling out in line of march, feeling somewhat huffy at the unkind treatment of the elements—some refractory cows and steers, loaded with blankets, tents and knapsacks, could be seen scampering over the plain, strongly protesting against being used as pack mules, and by vigorous kicks and plunges, to avoid capture, had scattered broadcast over the plain, the contents of their unwieldly burdens, holding high their heads as evidence of their triumphs, thereby causing uproars of laughter and. cheers as the result. Their example seemed contagious, for the pack mules witnessing their stubborn freaks, in turn play the oppossom, and refuse to go forward—as much as to say, that unless the others are brought back in the harness, they will not go, and in consequence there seemed to be a strong contest between their negro drivers and themselves as to the victory, thus imparting much merriment to the boys, and making up for the otherwise dismal state of affairs.

To-day we made very slow progress, on account of very miry roads, and the country was also very broken. Towards evening the rain ceased, and a strong wind took its place, cold and cutting in its nature, proving to our entire satisfaction that our clothing was too scanty to prevent its chilling effects; but shortly before dark, the clouds clearing away in the west, disclosed the blue sky, with white fleecy clouds slightly fringed with black, beautifully reflecting the last rays of the setting sun, together with an extensive and romantic view of hills and valleys in the distance, presented an enchanting scene, never to be forgotten; but the western horizon betokened a cold and cheerless night for us, which was fully realized, being far in the rear of advance division, we are satisfied of a night's work before us, and in ascending the rising bluffs in this section of the country, the train scarcely moves; in fact, every wagon has to be assisted by the troops up the hills and out of the deep cut ruts, previously made by the advance, and at such critical times as these, the teamsters do not spare their lungs, and the principal music of the occasion consisting in the sharp crackling of the whip, and the voice of the teamsters, hoarse with constant and vigorous exercise; and as one would listen, it would seem to be a contest of supremacy between them, and the cold wind, whose boisterous waves rolled over the tree tops with irresistible fury, searching every nook and corner unprepared for its reception; and all along the line of road, numerous fires, in fact, long lines of fence could be seen, rolling out its brilliant flame by the violence of the wind, and numerous groups of soldiers, huddling in close proximity to each other, endeavoring to absorb the heat in its rapid escape, as a temporary offset for the want of clothes. After crossing several steep and rugged bluffs, in this sluggish and disagreeable manner, we reached the valley, and soon made camp. It being 3 o'clock in the morning, and intensely cold, without any previous ceremony, we made our beds and rolled in for a few hours' rest—having traveled only eight miles in all. The advance of division reached camp sometime previous, and advance of 3d division overtaking us, on the bluffs previously spoken of, went into camp without waiting for us to get out of their way. Thus closed one of the most disagreeable days and nights of the campaign.

Nov. 22d: After a few hours rest, the assembly sounded and found us still hid in the folds of our blankets, and some of the troops already falling in, we suddenly emerged from our nests, and hastily packing our knapsacks, we followed in the wake of the army, and took our usual position in the ranks. The morning was intensely cold, having frozen the mud during the night an inch and a half thick. The wind was still asserting its prowess, as it rolled through the dark pine forests which gave back the echo of its unearthly and dismal sound.

The general appearance of things this morning, indicate a different soil and timber. We have just left the highlands, and this is our first introduction to the extensive pineries and swamps that characterize the southern portion of the Empire State of the South. This morning we make good time, and shortly afternoon we pass Gordon, the junction of the Extension Branch of the Georgia Central Railroad, and went into camp about one mile North-east of the same, having marched about eleven miles from the last encampment, and camped about 1 P. M. Here on the line of Railroad from Milledgeville to Gordon, and from there to the left of Macon, lay our whole army in line of march and battle ; and the destruction of the railroad is the next object [to be accomplished. The work of destruction of which was commenced to-day.

CHAPTER III.

Twentieth Corps Enter the Capital—Destruction of the Railroad—Engagement of the Fifteenth Corps with Hardee's Forces—Calm Succeeding Storm—Line of March of Seventeenth Corps—Troops in the Pineries—Soap Chandlers' Grand Opportunity—Description of Twisting Lever—Yankee Ingenuity—Important Lesson Taught—The Rush for Forage—Its Unmarketable Condition for Refined Purchasers—Grand Preparations for the Day's Wants—Opposition in the Front and Right of Way Disputed—Near Approach to the Oconee—Junction of Two Corps—Navigation of a Three Mile Swamp—Supply of New Conscripts—General Confiscation of Horses and Mules—The Reasons—Fearful Slaughter—Passage of the Stream—Grand Scene on Nearing Camp—The Union of the Two Corps Irresistible.

Nov. 23d: To-day nearly the whole of our Grand Army was engaged in the destruction of the railroad previously mentioned; our division being assigned to the task of destroying five miles of the same, in the direction of Milledgeville, which we successfully and thoroughly performed. The 20th corps entered the capital, appropriating extensive commissary stores to their use, and liberated a number of our prisoners found incarcerated there. While on the extreme right, a portion of the 15th army corps had a brisk little brush with Hardee's rebel forces, inflicting on them considerable injury. Night found the day's task of the army fully performed, and the line of railroad going to and from the rebel capital of Georgia was laid in ashes—the iron twisted in every conceivable shape, to prevent its future use. The artillery on the right was hushed to silence, and the whole army lay in silent repose, ready for its further advance on the morrow, having enjoyed a short respite from severe marching.

Nov. 24th: Revielle at 4 A. M., and being so far successful, the boys are in good spirits, and it was not long before all was activity and bustle throughout the entire camp. Having partaken of our breakfast, and packed our knapsacks for the day, about half past six A. M., we take up our line of march between Gordon and Miller, all the time keeping near the line of railroad, to tear up and destroy the same. So having in the capture of Atlanta and the destruction of the main channels of communication that led to the same the heart of the Confederacy cut, it becomes us now to sever some of the main arterial channels of circulation, in order to fully accomplish the final suppression of this gigantic struggle. To-day we passed a fair country, some considerable swamp, but rich plantations interspersed, the soil being for the most part sandy, but was informed of its being fertile, and some finely elevated in comparison with the low and dismal swamps. Regiments out of each brigade of the division, took their turn in tearing up the railroad and burning the same, as we progressed during the day; and toward night it became our regiment's turn to do its share, while the remainder went to camp. So passing the town of McIntyre, we went nearly two miles below the same, when we commenced to perform our allotted task. After its accomplishment, we reversed our course, going into camp on the west side of the railroad, near the town and about nine miles from Gordon, having marched about thirteen miles in all, but only nine in a direct course.

Nov. 25th: At the usual and customary hour this morning, the troops were all on the wing and actively engaged, long before the break of day, in making preparations for its subsequent duties. Our camps present a very different appearance, from its numerous fires in these dark and gloomy pineries, from what they did in the highlands. In the morning and evening the soldiers appear more like spectre forms, as seen through the thick haze of the black pine smoke, than anything else, as they move within its darkening folds, exposed to its unpleasant odor, and making it a profitable rendezvous for soap chandlers, could they suddenly be transported here with their very useful productions, as soap is in great demand, and it being a necessary article to soften the sombre film that envelopes the skin; and could you see many of the boys that have been untimely ordered out in line of march, you could scarcely distinguish them from the dusky African, were it not for the hair and lips, unmistakeable signs of the different races—in consequence soap is a very necessary article of forage in reference to the toilet.

To-day our division is in regular turns deployed on line of railroad again, vigorously engaged in its destruction. To those unacquainted with railroad burning, it being one of the many new phases of modern warfare, it may not be amiss to give a brief sketch of the same. In the first place, a regiment, brigade, or division, forms a line on either the right or left side of the railroad, as the case may be, and stacking arms, each brigade, regiment or company, takes its own length, according to its number of men. This being done, some take axes and break off the heads of the spikes that fasten the rail to the ties; others get poles for levers, and with the same, lift the irons from their beds; some get dry wood and rails to start the fires, while others pry up the ties, strongly imbedded in the soil from previous pressure. This being done, the next thing is, to pile the ties transversely, one upon the other, in layers of three, four, or five, as seems most convenient, making five or six layers in all, then piling two close together on the top, the irons are laid transversely on the top of same, so as to balance, then in like manner a tie or two is placed on the top of it, the stack being thus completed, dry wood and rails fill up the interstices, and the torch is applied. It does not take long for the raging flame with its subtle heat, to cause the ponderous iron to yield to its influence, and it can be seen gradually yielding itself in humble submission, the opposite ends gracefully touching the ground. But in order to completely disable it for future use, they take the plate or shoe, that connects the two irons together on the track, and with some telegraphic wire, fasten it on one end of a lever, then two taking their position, one on each end of the iron, they slide it on, and both turning at the same time in opposite directions, they completely turn it into the form of a screw; some take the irons red hot from the burning pile, and fold them around the nearest tree; and various other means and ways are resorted to, in fact a pleasant rivalry seems to incite the boys to various methods to see who can twist them in the most inconceivable shapes. To say the least the abettors of treason must ever remember the Yanks as not being at a loss for want of refined ingenuity, as the various waymarks throughout the heart of rebellion will long testify. As the fires are burning, some in order to take time by the forelock can be seen roasting meat; others making coffee, so as to enjoy more rest when they reach camp, while some are discussing the past history of this railroad and its probable future, and the spirit that charac-

terizes the boys in the exhibition of their destructive propensities, is entirely unlike
that which characterized former conquerors, or the goths and vandals that formerly
overrun Europe, but rather like the infliction of punishment by the master on a
very unruly and refractory scholar; and I am inclined to believe the South will
learn a lesson that indulgence never would have imparted.

About half past two, P. M., we went into camp for the night near Toonsboro—
having traveled in all about eleven miles, over a rather flat district, being sometimes very swampy, and then again somewhat broken, the nature of the soil being
similar to yesterday. And as we daily advance, each division of the corps takes
each their regular turn, and each does their regular and proper share of railroad
destruction. The weather for the past three or four days has been bracing—nights
frosty and cold—the days being favorable for marching, but it is moderating down
to a warmer temperature at present, and more in accordance with the general reputation of a southern clime. The boys being busy through the day and short of
rations, can be seen rushing out in various directions through the woods, in search
of domestic game and other necessaries indispensable to life and to maintain strength,
and late in the evening, returning with a fair supply of the swine tribe, swung on
their backs, not in a very marketable condition it is true, to invite the refined and
elite of society to purchase, were it exposed for sale in any of our public markets,
but still answers the purpose very well to stop the cravings of a soldier's appetite,
while others return as they went, feeling very hard toward the rebels, in meeting
with such poor success, and wisely claiming that the Confederacy, being the cause
of dragging them into its centre, should in consequence be compelled to supply
their every want. However, I have not seen any starve as yet, and it is generally
supposed we are doing well, if we escape the dread vulture.

Nov. 26th: This morning early, some of the boys, as if anxious to surprise the
lords of the hen roost, are on the alert unusually early, without waiting for the
bugle's shrill note, and are actively engaged in cooking the day's supplies in such
liberal quantities, as to openly avow their determed purpose to satisfy nature's every call, clearly proving the entire absence of penuriousness, when it can be had
" without money and without price," and a gormandizer whose taste is as the most
refined, and whose choice is not of the highest order—would open his eyes, and
swell his capacious stomach, and sharpen his cadaverous propensities, at the sight
of the liberal dishes served up in the army; for it is either feast or famine, enough
or nothing, with soldiers, whose life consists of two extremes in all its phases.
Yesterday there was some opposition in the front, as the advance neared the Oconee river, as if intending to dispute our passage across the same, or hinder our
progress, and cannonading could be distinctly heard at different hours of the day;
but this morning affairs seem to be more quiet again, and the duties of camp in
preparation for the day being attended to, at half past six, A. M., we fall in line of
march and move forward with our usual good success over a pretty fair country
about five miles, and their being an extensive swamp of about three miles between
here and the river, we turn in to the left for a temporary stay, while the road is
being made for the corps trains, and the pontoons are being laid. Here the Army
of the Tennessee again forms a junction, in order to cross the river at one and the
same time on two separate pontoon bridges, one for each corps, and laid within a
short distance of aach other. Toward night, our division began to move gradually
into line, but on account of the swamp in front, it was a slow and tedious job, and

occupied many hours in its passage. Occasionally, in passing along in conjunction with the train, a worn out mule could be seen swamped in the mud, arresting the progress of the whole train, and either would not, or could not get up. It is hard to witness, but the rough usage of the army so accustoms the boys to such scenes that every thing is made light of, and they can be heard to taunt the teamsters under such circumstances with their mules playing off sick; others that they are working for a discharge; which indeed they too often get, and a final one; for when they cannot succeed in extricating them, the wagoners leave them to the mercy of the crushing wheels of those that follow after, and thus they are finally discharged for disabilities received in service, and their final statement,—died in action! I suppose is made out, as the last epitome of their previous existence, and their places filled up again in the supply of new conscripts; thus the trains are constantly needing recruits, as well as the rank and file. But after several hours struggling in and through the miry swamps, and the number of casualties in the train being numerous, we finally reached the river in our turn well bespattered with its slimy contents. But there is one feature of army life carried out to the letter at every unfordable stream, which will occupy a short space in its description. It is invariably the case that in traveling through the enemy's country, all classes of foragers make it their ruling object to be always on the alert for horses and mules, which they find in large numbers, in going through such a country as Georgia. Bummers, headquarter clerks, orderlies, and various other classes following the army are also on the same track. In consequence of the same, between the principal streams they accumulate on the army very fast, and in a short time become numerous; this being the case—the train constantly losing mules from their numbers, or some becoming worn out and unfit for duty—a strong guard is detailed by order of division quartermaster, to stop and take all the horses and mules found in the possession of those that are not entitled to them, from their position, for a better use. And this for a variety of reasons. 1st. It consumes too much time and hinders the progress of the army across the river, which is an important item in a large army like ours. 2d. It encourages the evacuation of too many men from the ranks. 3d. It is often a difficult job at all times to secure a sufficient quantity of corn and fodder to feed such an overplus of horse flesh, and were they retained, it would cause many necessary and serviceable horses and mules to go hungry, that the useless and worthless would consume. 4th. It is the means of throwing out from the trains and other parts of the army, the useless and worn out, replacing them with serviceable ones, thus making the army much more effective. This being done all the unserviceable and useless are either knocked in the head or shot at a proper and convenient place near by. This is a very unpleasant duty for those upon whom it falls, but like many other disagreeable duties, it is a necessity and must be done—the object being to cripple the enemy in every possible resource; and should we leave the cripples and worn out stock, they would endeavor to recuperate them for future use. It therefore becomes indispensable to put them out of the way, thus sometimes causing the slaughter of hundreds at a single crossing. About 10 P. M. we all succeeded in effecting a crossing, and moving two miles beyond, through a flat and level road to a more elevated piece of land, where we went into camp about 11 P. M., having marched during the day and night about eleven miles in all. As we coursed our way along the line of road leading to the camp—the vast numbers of camp-fires as seen all around in the front, rising some

—4

above the other—presented the appearance of a grand amphitheatre, looking cheerful and inviting, as one viewed the great semi-circle of dazzling fires, when issuing
from the dark background of our position.   To the soldier weary from the toils of
the day, the camp with its cheerful fires, ever seems an inviting guest, and the
manner in which it is always hailed, proves the fact; and in the present instance,
as soon as the troops caught a glimpse of its unerring indication, resounding cheers
were heard all along the line, repeated and hearty, thus showing their full appreci-
ation of its inviting appearance.   The 2d corps having previously met for the passage of the river, camp in near proximity to each other, as if to improve and enjoy
a friendly visit, and present a strong front to he foe, and in unison are almost irresistible.

CHAPTER IV.

FROM THE OCONEE TO MILLEN.

Promptitude of Musicians—The Planter's Accusation—Acknowledgement of the John-nies—Sherman's Military Embrace—Morning Details—Tricks of Stragglers—Sherman Changes from Left to Right Centre—His letter of Distinction and Policy—Night Picketing—The Sleeping Giant—Amusing Scenes in Navigating Swamps—Foraging Regulations—Passage of Rocky Creek—Arrival at Sebastopol—Destruction of the Depot and Stores—Army Beacons—Sherman's Fearful Scourge—The Rebel Congressman—Skedaddling Tact of the Rebels—Arrival at Millen—Its Description and Destruction—Contrasted Institutions of the 2d Sections.

Nov. 27th: The lateness of the hour we reach camp, makes no difference in the next morning's rising; for as near the alloted hour as possible, the martial airs and shrill notes of the bugle can always be heard at the proper time, and the idea of thinking that some morning they may forget to raise the customary alarm, and so allow you to enjoy an extended nap, is entirely out of question; for every regimental head quarter guard, always receives imperative orders to arouse the musicians and buglers at a given hour, and they seldom allow you to take advantage of them in the matter of rising at the assigned time. So at 4 A. M. they can be heard in every direction sounding the alarm, neither sparing the lungs or the drum sticks, and it would sometimes seem as though they were endeavoring to make unusual efforts to swell the notes if possible a few keys higher than common, as if to give the troops no excuse as to a timely warning; but whether they arise or not in order to secure breakfast, previous to departure, when the signal to fall in is raised, there is no time to wait, no palliation of excuses, but whether breakfast has been disposed of or not, all must be in ther proper places; and those that are not ready must take matters as they are, not as they would like. Ere the break of day we began to take up our line of march on the highway, and the roads and country being pretty favorable for travel, we make good time, and glide over the surface more rapidly than usual. Yesterday and to-day, we marched on the west side of the railroad, and all going forward with alacrity and success. About 11 o'clock, A. M. we went into camp, near Tennille Station, having marched about ten miles from last encampment. The day was warm and pleasant, more like summer than autumn, and presented a striking contrast to us in comparison to what we were accustomed to in the North; although the planters accuse us of bringing the cold along with us wherever we go, as they often declare it unusually cold near the line, and around the outskirts of the Yankee army. Probably our manner, (if not the weather), is often very chilling, and the Johnnies sometimes acknowledge receiving from us a very warm introduction, and subsequently, a too generous outflow of warmth, and a too liberal supply of rations, more than they want no doubt; but not more than they need while in open rebellion against all lawful authority and former good treatment. They also often acknowledge that we are too anxious to embrace them, and for that purpose they accuse us of paying especial attention to our flanks, compelling them very often to retire very unceremoniously, without giving us their customary salute, and betake themselves to a more convenient place of safety, to escape the tightening cords of *Sherman's military embrace*; and like the Norwegian in the dark recesses of the forest, with an untimely introduction to the grizzly monsters that infest those regions, they would prefer escape from its peculiar hug, if possible ; but if unable to do the same, the hidden dagger is withdrawn for defense; but escape is far preferable, if it is only possible.

To-day the 15th army corps is in camp about two miles to our right, and a part of it is deployed on line of railroad, and exercising what phrenologists would term the organ of destruction, and cultivating the muscular powers in following the same vocation that engaged our attention for several previous days, allowing us the privilege to rest for the remainder of the day, to prepare ourselves for future action. Accordingly we make the best of our opportunity and attend to our sanitary conditions, which is an important item in our wandering life, and indispensable to health and comfort.

Nov. 28th : Having enjoyed what in raiding life we consider *a good rest*, and nature favoring us with genial warmth during the night, we feel more supple this morning, and less inclined than sometimes to quarrel with our circumstances, and the boys seem generally on the alert in seasonable time to prepare for the order of march ; and after the little minor affairs have been attended to, and the morning meal dispensed with, the customary details are made from the ranks as usual, thus in order: 1st. Regimental headquarter guard, whose duty it is through the day to march in the extreme rear of the regiment, to prevent and pick up if possible, all its stragglers. 2d. A provost guard to march in the rear of brigade—each regiment of the brigade furnishing its proportionate number—whose duty it is to pick up all stragglers from the brigade. 3d. A division provost guard to march in the rear of the whole division, to pick up all stragglers from the command, furnished in the same ratio from each regiment ; but at present it is found more convenient, less trouble, and equally effective—to make a permanent detail for the same, to act in that capacity during the campaign, reporting to their commands at night, and returning to their respective posts of duty every morning. But it must not be supposed that with all this precaution, every straggler is picked up, or that none escape their detection, for the troops often seemed determined, if possible, to out do their commanders in ingenuity, and the tighter the screws are turned on, the more they often set their wits to work to counteract it, for there are those in the army, who like the fabled Phœnix, are seldom seen, and the greater the attempt to prevent their egress from the ranks, the more anxious they are to escape, and like the slippery eel they easily elude the grasp ; others tax their ingenuity to the utmost in framing statements to account for their absence from the ranks, while some, with a dexterity of action, that becomes natural and easy, distort their appearance in various ways, presenting the appearance of a genuine convalescent, to accomplish their original purpose, to avoid an official inquiry, and it must be confessed that they often too well succeed in their object; but with all the cunning and curious manœuvers resorted to by the rank and file, to accomplish their object, yet fewer outrages occur in our army than in any other of such magnificent size. The day has been excessively warm for the season of the year, and as we pushed our way along with a rapidity seldom equaled by any army, the perspiration could be seen to ooze freely from the pores of the skin, and the country being pretty level, with extensive young pineries on either side of us most of the way, it would seem as though the atmosphere was retaining an unusual excess of heat, causing a too liberal expenditure of moisture from the system, similar to a steam bath, for our under clothing pretty well testified the effects of our going through a hot air bath. General Sherman having moved from the left centre of the army, to the right centre of the same, in the afternoon the old veteran took a field review of that portion of his army represented by the 17th army corps as they passed along the road, and although the boys sometimes think he handles them very roughly in constant field service, yet they are warmly attached to him, and speak of him in some very familiar terms, such as the following: as they pass in full view of him, one will remark: "There stands the daddy of this army;" another will say, "There's our old dad;" others say, "There's old Billy;" and numbers use the appellation of, "Crazy Bill"—not in anyway of disrespect, but claim it to be a time honored title among his old companions, in their particular distinguishment of genuine respect and honor for his abilities. However, many of the boys have their own peculiar title of dignity and honor for him. And although the "Iron Duke and victor of Waterloo" is distinguished for his numerous and lengthy titles, as badges of honor for his indomitable energy, skill, perseverance and success, by the nation that fully appreciated his services,—yet I very much doubt whether they would bear a strict comparison with those cherished and endearing titles spontaneously conferred upon General Sherman by the veterans that have followed him through many a battlefield. And they will accomplish more and suffer more under him than under any other man in the field; and all moves made by him are considered indispensable to success, and the boys think he would not make them for any other purpose. One feature of the general they think deserves the highest credit, and that is, they all firmly believe he is not so ambitious for fame or a name, as for success in the speedy suppression of this fratricidal strife: thus constantly pursuing the enemy when once routed, to prevent as much as possible their future intrenchment, and striking where least expected some distant point, thereby compelling the evacuation of other strongholds, that would otherwise cause a too liberal effusion of blood and sacrifice of life, and the success of the past year fully proves the entire success of our commanding general's policy, which for brilliancy, celerity of movement and success, is unsurpassed in history.

Our division being in advance of corps, 3d division in the centre, and 4th division in the rear to-day, our division went into camp about 3 P. M., near General Sherman's headquarters, having marched during the day about 16 miles. A company of the 39th Ohio, and company B from our regiment, furnished pickets for the brigade, which were immediately taken out and posted in front of our command. It is necessary to state here, that on the line of march as well as in close contact with the enemy, each brigade, division and corps, pickets and guards its own front, and at whatever hour of the day or night a brigade reaches camp, pickets are immediately posted from a mile to a mile and a half in advance, forming their line in conformity with the form of camp, thus always presenting an unbroken front to the enemy, and ever prepared for a sudden dash or attack of the foe, and thereby giving the entire camp sufficient time for preparation, should they wish to bring on a general engagement with us in the field. But night steals on apace, and each division having reached the terminus of their day's march the tattoos of the different and numerous regiments announce the near approach of the hour for repose. And listening while alone on picket to the various notes, as their final vibrations fell on the ear of a silent listener, while a vast army lays in in its extensive recess, gradually yielding itself up to the slumbering fold of Morpheus, as the last echoing sounds of their voices are hushed to silence, and the many sad reminiscences connected with its very recent history, as exhibited in the fury and storm of battle, and all the conflicting passions of their nature were called into vigorous exercise, it presented a grand theme for meditation, and a striking contrast one to the other. I could not in my thoughts but compare them to a sleeping giant. How innocent and harmless they now appear as they are locked in night's pleasant embrace ; but should the wily foe now raise the dread alarm, how mighty and sudden would be the transition from rest to labor, from repose to action, from calm to storm, from the pleasant dreams and visions of sleep, to the stern and dread realities of mortal combat, when the leaden hail would be traveling with the swiftness of electricity, to and fro through the atmospheric air, like so many winged messsengers of death ; and when the horrid yells and hisses of those terrible shells, as they issue from the rifled monsters of modern destruction, are thinning the ranks of those found in its dread pathway.   But the former is more to be courted than the latter, and peace far preferable to war, as the desolating experience of a four years' conflict will abundantly testify, in the mourning and sorrow caused in almost every household in the land.

Nov. 29th : To-day we take the rear of corps, our brigade center of division, and regiment in the lead of brigade, and the third and fourth division being in our advance, taking some time to get fairly under way, our division was not fairly on the march until near 10 o'clock A. M. And it being the intention to make good time to-day, upon the clearance of the road, there is a general endeavor on the part of the troops to improve the time, but the country being more flat and swampy than any previously past or experienced, we meet with more obstacles than usual as we encounter the swamps adjoining the head waters of the Cannoochee river, and toward dusk we crossed the same near Codwick station. It consists of several pretty considerable sized streams, much resembling creeks, with swamps and flat sheets of water interspersed, while on either side large swamps are attached making it troublesome and disagreeable to effect a passage, which is invariably attended with wet feet, and occasionally from accident the entire person becomes submerged in the stream, which sometimes proves an unfortunate occurrence, for instead of extending sympathy to such poor persons, it is generally made the subject of much merriment to his comrades, who take the favored opportunity to enjoy a joke and laugh at his expense. Another source of imparting much pastime to the ranks, is this: Each company in the regiment being allowed a pack mule, or two, according to their number, to carry all the extra rations or forage if there be any, and blankets for those not able to carry them, although but few enjoy that privilege apart from the driver, and their mess, or their particular friends, and it very often turns out that they have very unwieldly burdens imposed on them. Sometimes men are detailed from the ranks to lead them, and in other cases negroes are taken for that purpose, and not being so dexterous as our white boys, nor as ingenious in piloting over the streams and swamps, and the beds of the streams not of the smoothest kind, it often turns out that some projecting root, or stump, or deep cavity, plunges the mules with their burdens and drivers in the depths of the stream, completely baptizing them with water, but they shortly rise above the surface of the sluggish stream, and grope their way out from such an uncomfortable position ; but previous to their exit they have to undergo and listen to the merriment and jokes freely indulged in at their expense, besides enjoying the prospect of testing Hydropathic treatment in the form of wet blankets at night, unless fortunate enough to reach camp in sufficient time to dry them, which is not always the case; and the rank and file in crossing upon poles and rails, laid in every conceivable shape, need the nerve and dexterity of a Blondin to avoid contact with the watery element, and wanting in this many enjoy the unwelcome treat of immersion, and when you hear constant screams and hearty yells and laughs, you may take it for granted that it is at the expense of those who have met with disaster and temporary defeat in crossing those dark and unfrequented byways, but after considerable effort on the part of the troops and train and a prolonged and vigorous exercise of the lungs in incessant cheers and screams, to enliven the passage of this dark and dismal recess, (for it is after night has set in), we emerged from the gloomy shades, and moving some distance beyond, we went into camp for the night, about 8 o'clock, having marched about fifteen miles during the day's journey, and camping near what is called Rocky—but which might be more appropriately called Softy—creek, as in its general aspect it presents more the appearance of a continuous swamp than creek. This evening camp was a welcome guest to us all, as most of the troops were pretty weary, and the lower extremities of their persons being thoroughly saturated with water. It is not long before the cheerful camp fires light up the dreary appearance of things and glance in which direction you please, all can be seen busily engaged in drying and cooking at one and the same time, as it is very expedient and necessary to glean as much time as possible for rest and sleep, and a number of little chores to be nightly attended to, makes it imperative to expedite matters as much as possible, and ere much time is consumed, the general hubbub which just now was the chief characteristic of camp, is hushed to silence, and the reigning quietness which pervades the grand pavilion, proves that the scenes of another day are swept away by life's current into oblivion's hidden ocean, ne'er to be recalled.

Nov. 30th: At an early hour this morning, we were aroused as usual, and informed that our toils and marches had not ceased, and the necessity of another round forced itself on our minds as an imperative duty, and if we would secure breakfast previous to departure we must be up and doing, or the privilege will not be granted, as military law is like wind and weather, that waits for no one; so making the best of our bargain we emerge from our not very stylish beds, and set to work with a will; but the effects of yesterday makes itself to be felt upon us, causing our movements rathy gouty and stiff; but feelings are not allowed to be our guide or guage as to the distance to be travelled, and being fully up to the real condition of affairs we think it best to urge matters in order to secure our breakfast, and comfortably pack our knapsacks for convenient transportation, as it is a very necessary item, for the manner of packing the same makes quite a difference in the matter of ease for its support during the day's march. And after the morning's duties are performed, and its numerous details attended to, we take up our line of march, and before proceeding further with the subject, one matter I must notice by the way, which to many unacquainted with military details and arrangements is a mystery, and that is foraging regulations. It becomes a matter of surprise to the masses of civilians, as to how an army of such proportions as ours, can daily prosecute its journey, through an enemy's country, and yet at the same time collect the vast amount of supplies necessary to sustain life and strength, for while it takes a

very large amount to supply 70,000 to 80,000 men irrespective of all the hangers
on, negroes and refugees, and others gathered up as we daily advance, yet in doing
so, we do not furnish provisions for much over one half of what really belongs to
the army, when you come to include all the mules, horses and horned stock, that is
embraced in the cavaly branch of the service, as well as headquarter, ordnance and
supply trains, together with a large number of mounted men, requiring horses and
mules in all the various branches of the service, making in full told, an immense
number. Yet such is the case, that in the prosecution of our journey through the
present campaign, we not only accomplished the task, but made a daily average of
some fifteen miles march in addition. Consequently every morning, company foragers, are regularly detailed to forage, each for their respective companies ; and all
the various headquarters from General Sherman's down to regimental, have each
their separate foragers for the same, and all detachments and squads in the different
branches of the service are each allowed their forage details. In our present campaign two or three from each company of the regiment was detailed daily, but having to carry the forage as well as their own accoutrements, we had often to go hungry for want of grub, and were often compeled to turn foragers on our own hook,
after reaahing camp or by sliding out of the ranks during the day, but sometimes
these foot foragers by getting early the start of us, would move far in advance, collect what supplies they could, and bringing it by the wayside, waiting for the arrival
of their respective companies, and distribute the same, and killing a lot of hogs
and dividing them up, the boys would each take a portion carrying the same on the
barrels of their muskets for want of better transportation. And the numerous little
markets of meat presented to view by the roadside, in our line of travel, formed a
very unique spectacle to behold, but not a very attractive one to a very tasty be-
holder, as there is not much ceremony paid to their slaughter. But the success
necessary to a liberal supply of forage, depends principally on two things. 1st. The
division commander. 2d. In abundant transportation. For if the division commander considers it necessary, he has the power to allow a forage wagon or two to
each regiment, for the express purpose of carrying regimental forage, and in such a
provision should there be an overplus for the present, it is retained for future use,
and should any of the troops pick up any by the way, from any other source they
can; take it there for transportation. Thus by this simple arrangement they can
be properly supplied, and by the same prevent much waste, that often otherwise
takes place, and some division commanders there are, who are thus much thoughtful
although our division in the present campaign was not so fortunate, and had to do
our own toting as well as foraging. Sometimes the boys are lucky enough to find
transportation for their stuff, as I have noticed in another chapter, and are at such
times independent of Government transportation. But past experience has sug-
gested the necessity and propriety of mounted foragers, as they are far more efficient
than ones on foot, although during our present campaign, this provision was perhaps not thought of; for every campaign proves more effective in organization than
any previous one, as experience makes perfect and gives us the past upon which to
improve. In short, I believe upon the whole, that more provision is collected after
reaching camp than previously, for if the rations are wanting and not furnished
from the proper source, the boys are determined to make a raise themselves, and
for this purpose I have known them after reaching camp, to travel miles to procure
the same and divide the spoils on their return. The cause of a poor and niggardly

supply is not in the country we pass, always, nor the fault of department and corps commanders but in some subordinate officials, who are thus much wanting in attention to those placed under their charge, and the only redress sought under such circumstances is to take the matter in their own hands, and make up for the deficiency. But in order to secure corn and fodder for the trains of the army, a definite number of wagons not loaded during the day, strike out on either the right or left side of the road, with a sufficient guard, in search of the same, and at night return with supplies sufficient for the whole train, and cannoniers, orderlies, and every other class of mounted men, go far in the advance, and securing their sacks of corn and bundles of fodder, they bring them to the roadside and await the coming up of the wagons to receive it, and large numbers not fortunate enough to secure it through the day, in the evening when reaching camp, can be seen rushing in every direction in search of what they need, and so by resorting to various means and taking various directions, ere night folds us with its shady mantle, all are liberally provided. But I am safe in concluding that the country left in our rear daily, is pretty much cleared of all it contained, leaving the inhabitants to conclude that they had experienced a human plague, or at least, that some unusually ravenous creatures had committed a general depredation, and passed on, without asking the privilege or right of way. But to return, we had not proceeded far on our journey, before we encountered Rocky creek, previously noticed, and to us it proved a difficult crossing on foot, as we had to cross on narrow poles and brush, and small trees previously felled by the pioneer corps, most of us experiencing a disagreeable foot bath, ere we effected its passage, which occupied some considerable time, and having succeeded in clearing in full the head waters of the Cannouchee, we traveled several miles over a very flat country, of which the term, "well watered" could be strictly applied, as water and pine trees seemed apparently to reign supreme, they being the principal characteristics presented to view in this dark and dense wilderness. Having been confined to the west side of the railroad for several days, and bearing off some distance from the same to effect the passage of the streams and swamps previously described ; about noon we filed left and bore off in an oblique direction until nearly night when we neared the headwaters of Ogeechee. This proved another dismal swamp to us, but fortunately in pursuing the rebels very close, we partially saved the bridge spanning the main channel of the stream. They had set fire to it, but timely extinguishing it, it was not damaged so much, but that a little labor sufficiently repaired it for the passage of infantry, while a pontoon bridge was laid over the main channel for the trains to cross on. Groping and struggling in the adjoining swamps consequent on the stream for some time, with the same usual musical symphonies in full blast, we finally reached the bridge and crosing over the main stream, we soon succeeded in reaching the railroad at Sebastopol station, and moving about one and a half miles below the same, on the east side of the road, we encamped on a spacious plantation, about 7 P. M., having marched fully fourteen miles or more. Here we found a very fine station house, full of corn, a fine lot of lumber and railroad iron, with other stores, all of which was consigned to the flames, it being one of the many evidences of stern dealing with the perpetrators of treason and open rebellion ; and only one of the wholesome and numerous strokes of Sherman's peculiar form and manner of treating with the enemies of our humane Government.

Thus in the last few days march on the west side of the railroad until we again

—5

reached the same, our line of march described an irregular triangle, taking the line of the road as the base or hypotheneuse. The boys, being weary, soon turn in, and forgetting the past, not yet obliterated from their memories, they calmly resign themselves without a struggle to the goddess of night, trusting implicitly to the shelter of her timely mantle, as its sombre folds noiselessly fell in silent protection over their yielding forms.

DEC. 1st: Having secured what is absolutely necessary and indispensable to good health and the proper recuperation of the wasting energies of nature from constant daily waste, in the vigorous prosecution of a work that requires no little amount of physical strength, and determination of purpose to daily, and often nightly, sternly face the difficult tasks that are required of us, we are found as usual, like clock-work, ready to accomplish the part to be assigned us for the day. And we are early apprised of what is in store for us, for the returning rays of twilight have scarcely been recognised, ere the clanking of irons can distinctly be heard not far in the distance, and in taking a backward view of the state of affairs, dense volumes of smoke can already be seen looming up in massive billows to the skies, it being a most truthful indication of the whereabouts of the different portions of Sherman's army. As all along our war trail through the State, when on rising ground, we could see the plain indications of the line of travel of those corps to our right and left, by the sky beacon always so prominent night and day, forcibly reminding one of our outward resemblance to Israel in the wilderness, as by day the "cloudy pillar" of each army corps could be constantly seen at a distance, while at night the numerous fires of the different camps, beautifully reflect our exact position, in golden hues, making the appearance to fitly represent the "pillar of fire," as it lights up the horizon with its cheerful reflection.

About 7 o'clock P. M., our whole division moved out and was deployed on line of railroad in order to accomplish its destruction. This being our morning's task, the boys all worked with determined perseverance, and ere the meridian sun poured down its midday heat, miles of railroad had been made to pay part of the costly bill of treason in the complete destruction of its costly material. As we advance down the line, already passing through the fiery ordeal, and being compelled on account of the presence of swamps on either side, to walk in close proximity to the fires, we find it difficult to bear the intense heat of the long range of fiery furnaces now in full blast, as we hastily rush past every burning pile. The day was also very warm, thus adding as it were fuel to the flame, and causing the perspiration to flow in liberal profusion down the reddened cheeks of those who may be strictly termed, Sherman's fearful scourge,—as the Empire State can well testify that they proved a fearful besom to her sacred soil, in leaving their century marks in a long and wide strip that marks the war trail of our irresistible advance with a fell swoop that bore everything before us. Shortly afternoon we left the railroad to our right, and ere many miles advance, we encountered the great cypress swamp, which we found very ugly and difficult to navigate ; but after severe exertion and our usual cold water bath we effected its passage, and passed over some extensive plantations, in a good state of cultivation and improvement, and brought up in camp not far from the same, on the right side of the road in an extensive pinery not far from General Sherman's headquarters, which was established at the large and stately mansion of a Mr. Jones, who I was informed, was a member of the rebel congress, and who had made good his timely exit, previous to our arrival. The architectural design of the mansion much resembled the form of a large public building, having like many of the dwellings of the Southern States, large corinthian columns in front. It was three stories high with a square roof, while in the center of the same was a square enclose surrounded with a balustrade, thereby enabling the owner to enjoy a full and extensive view of his broad possessions. The whole design forming a correct expression of genuine aristocratic proclivities. It was between this proud mansion and Cushingville station, three-fourths of a mile below us, that we encamped for the night. The honorable gentleman just referred to, previous to his departure, had secluded large stocks of cured hams, shoulders, and side meat, which unhappily for the owner, the quick scenting Yankee had ferretted out, and as is usual in such cases, appropriated it to their especial benefit; a lot of valuable silver ware was found by others, and a sharp witted old negro left in charge of a lot of hidden mules and horses, had concluded that we were more deserving of them than his rebel fugitive master, took the express liberty to turn them over to the use of Uncle Sam, thereby proving his genuine loyalty, in strongly protesting against treason, and some of the boys endeavoring to test his allegiance, he would prove the same by referring to his recent act, thus silencing all accusation in the prosecution of his case ; and I would here intimate by the way, that previous to the exit of our army from this spot previously consecrated to the object of rebellion, it had dearly paid the sacrificial cost of its unruly owner, and should he ever return to his once happy homestead, it will impart to him a silent lesson on the impressive results of the inauguration of civil strife, and the heavy cost for such a serious undertaking, but he is only one among many that has paid the dear bought experience of that action that plunged a once truly happy and prosperous people into the deadly contest of civil strife, and its subsequent prosecution being conducted on a grand yet terrible scale, they must expect terrible results.

Dec. 2d: For several days past we have experienced exceedingly warm weather for the time of year, and this morning we moved ont at the usual hour under the same favorable auspices that have marked our invariable success. Our advance did not travel far before meeting with opposition in the front, and the boys being so accustomed to success, take but little notice of their faint demonstrations, and push right on as though nothing was in their way, and the rebels taking the timely hint, thus respectfully given them, skedaddle with their usual dexterity and success in the matter of retreat and flight, and it is an undisputed fact that they have become perfect adepts in the science, and practiced its profession until it has almost become a second nature to them; although the boys sometimes wish that they would prepare themselves for a short stay, in order to afford them a short respite from what they sometimes term a wild goose chase ; but although they manage to keep up their reputation for retreat, and of presenting back instead of front views of their persons ; yet they sometimes squat themselves down to some purpose, and inflict some damage on us by so doing, but always manage to secure a loophole for a timely exit when pushed, or as the Southern ladies have It, when they see our "flinkers" manifest their appearance, they then go it their best in order to win the race in accordance with the old lines,

"That he that safe can get away,
May live to fight some other day,"
"But he that by 'Long Tom' is slain,
Shall never live to fight again."

After traveling some distance over a favorable country on the left side of the railroad, we stumble on another of those swampy bogs, peculiar to the level lands and pineries of Southern Georgia, and effecting a successful passage, we reached one of the main tributaries of the Ogeechee, near the railroad. On reaching the iron road of modern improvement, we marched directly down the same about two miles, when we reached Millen, the junction of the Augusta branch of the Savannah and Macon railroad, and went a short distance south-east of the same, where we squatted for the night, about 4 o'clock P. M., having marched about twelve miles from the last encampment.

Millen is principally noted for its lengthy depot, and numerous switches; it also contained some large cotton warehouses, whose exterior was not the most attractive to the eye. A few very inferior looking dwellings, and a small saloon, but this important junction could not even boast of a second or third-rate hotel—it being a conclusive argument in favor of free, in comparison, to slave labor; and in our march through the State, we passed a number of sites favorable to the growth of a large town, but from want of free institutions and northern enterprise, remained like a tree stunted in its growth by rough usage and bad treatment, and every year manifests more clearly, that effeminacy which characterizes the absence of a healthy and enterprising spirit so predominant, as the result of a dominant aristocracy, but it is to be hoped that the billowy upheavings of this vast human crater that has been disgorging itself for the past four years, will bring about a different state of things in the South; for it is self-evident that the contact of the two sections, brought about by this war, has demonstrated most clearly the superiority of the North to the South in a variety of ways. For in all of our meanderings through its sacred soil, we have never seen a fair display of that characteristic ingenuity which seems the peculiar birthright of free institutions, displayed in such unparalleled ingenuity as witnessed in the North. For the simple implements of husbandry here, antedate the appearance of things a century past, and improvements that have long since been superseded by better ones in the North, have scarcely had the privilege of an introduction in the South; and language that has long since become obsolete in the North, in the South is in popular use, and proves clearly, that Mr. Webster's vast labors for the benefit of the English language, have met with but a cold reception at the best. But I have no doubt as to a decided improvement in the future, and am safe in concluding that the many contacts of the past, although hostile in their intention and purpose, will eventually work out its favorable results, and lead to the full acknowledgement of free and liberal institutions, and to the explosion of those fogyish theories that have bound its victims for long years in their enthralmnnt, and conduct their emancipated spirits to sure, certain and speedy triumph.

DEC. 3d: This morning is ushered in as usual, with no particular indications of a different state of things from what is commonly witnessed in our every day life, save that the spacious depot is being considerably reduced from its previous size, as the broad and livid sheets of flame encircle its massive proportions, rendering its appearance magnificent, yet awful to look upon, as its expansive flames were making themselves felt at the warehouses in near proximity, and it was not long before everything in the shape of a building, was lapped in the destructive element, and proud Augusta flanked out of her railroad communication by its main arterial channel of life, is left to mourn her present loneliness in painful separation from a sister city, with whom she had frequent intercourse up to a recent date, but the daily advance of our army is constantly causing such separations, and so completely isolating and bleeding the central portion of the sham Confederacy, that but little life is left, and the hearts of those that were once exultant and defiant now droop over the sad results of their own folly and madness, and learn when too late, the fearful cost of war and its concomitant fruits.

The surroundings of this junction are anything but attractive, and its impoverished site and general exterior very commonplace. However, its easy occupation was a matter of surprise to us, as we expected to have a contest for its possession, but securing so pleasant an introduction and such easy access, we have concluded to render it useless and abortive to the conspirators during the continuation of the struggle; and to make good our conclusions, we are early up and doing, and no great length of time expires before we bid a lasting farewell to our recent camp, and deploy on the line of railroad, not to skirmish with a conceded foe, but to destroy a road previously consecrated to rebellion, and a highway that is considered of much importance in modern warfare, and a few short hours presents those numerous switches and the long line of road below the same, a burning wreck. Perhaps the reader may think all this a useless destruction of public property; but such is not the case, as the more we can divide their armies, by destroying the channels which facilitate their rapidly collecting together, the more thoroughly are we sapping the life of their dangerous and destructive intentions, and so bewilder them in their secret and diabolical conclaves, as to render its useless and imperfect consummation a complete failure, and the entire success that has crowned Sherman's plans, proves the happy result.

CHAPTER V.

FROM MILLEN TO SAVANNAH.

Preparations for a Storm—A Volunteer not a Regular—Sherman's Troops in line of March—A News Depot—Case of Assault and Battery—Hostile Demonstrations— Rush to the Front—Retrograde Movement—Officers want of Interest—Provisional Gardens—Georgia's loss in Cotton—Wholesale Destruction—Formidable Obstructions—The peculiar Music of the Occasion—Our appearance on emerging from the Swamps—Ire of the Johnnies as we near the City—Corduroying Roads—Bummers Butting against the Foe—In quest of Game—Army Butchering—A novel method of Trapping—Reaching the Rebel Works at Savannah—Rebels keenly alive to the Occasion.

During the morning our whole division prosecuted the destruction of the road, and the remainder of the day we marched alternately on the east and west side of the road as far as Scarboro station, over a passable country, slightly undulating, with intervening swamps. Here we reversed our course about one mile on the east side of the road over a very extensive plantation, in order to secure a roomy position for the establishment of camp; making the distance travelled by us about nine and a half miles—irrespective of railroad burning—and camped for the night about dusk.

The day was very warm, as well as several previous ones; but the appearance of the horizon this evening indicates a change of affairs, and betokens a liberal supply of aqueous fluid, and the boys calmy viewing the threatening state of its appearance, have concluded to defend themselves againsts its attack; and as soon as their arms are stacked, they could be seen running in every direction after the necessary poles on which to stretch their tents, which consist of two uprights with crotches at the top, set according to the width of the tent, with a pole horizontally laid across the top to support the tent and on which it is stretched, and fastened with short stakes to the ground. Thus the military mansion of the soldier is completed. Some fasten a covering over one of the gables, being guided by the direction of the wind as to which end, and when thus secured, they bid defiance to wind and weather, and sleep as securely and contented as in the most costly mansion of the land. It is only when threatened with rain, or when arriving early in camp, that the boys pitch their tents when daily prosecuting their journey; but when arriving late at our nightly goal, we simply spread our blankets on the ground without any further ceremony, and at length night drops her curtain over the scene, and the boys willingly accept the proffered protection.

Dec. 4. The morning was clear and pleasant and the air very bracing, from the fall of pleasant showers during the night, and at an early hour we awoke to a full sense of our existence, and all was timely engaged in preparing for what was in store. It is true that the rank and file are not generally supposed to know anything before hand, but like a machine, wait to be set in motion, and not a move must be made in the line before the command is given, and then a prompt obedience is required; but it is sometimes very difficult to mold the volunteer to that rigid stiffness, and to hold them in that abeyance that characterizes the regular service. He is a free volunteer and has proffered his services for the salvation of his country, not his free and easy manners—the spontaneous productions of the heart—but simply his services to the best of his abilities, retaining that which he considers the peculiar birthright of his life, and acquired in the cradle of liberty. You may train him until he becomes an adept in the performance of military tactics, and train him in all the minutiæ of military discipline, but he is still the same volunteer. In fact you may train and drill him over and over again, but you cannot obliterate that which he inherited; and a commander whose demeanor is austere and overbearing, they cannot tolerate, and the farther the distance that separates him from them the better, as such a spirit cannot command their respect or toleration.

It is in the fury and storm of battle that the brave and patriotic volunteer can be seen to be fully appreciated and properly valued. He fights and bares his devotional breast to the chances of battle, not because he has to fight and kill, but because his fatherland is in danger and needs firm protection and support, that he braves the fury of the leaden storm. Fighting is not his profession. He only does it from the absolute necessity of the case, in order to suppress anarcy and civil strife, and to maintain the preservation of free and liberal institutions.

As we are early forming in line of march, continuous cheers and yells can be heard as usual, as some comical exhibition of action or form calls forth roars of laughter and ringing hurrahs along the line of our command—and it is a peculiar and open characteristic of the volunteer. From the indications of this morning as we briskly move out, we are to make considerable headway to-day. All seems favorable; the roads and country good, and nothing apparently in the way to stop our rapid advance, and ere many hours have passed, we have left several miles in our rear. But it must not be understood that Sherman's raiders (as we are sometimes called) make as graceful an appearance on the line in our raiding excursions, as on dress parade or exhibitional reviews. Far from it. If we do not look as stylish and starched, yet it is very evident we look far more dangerous, and so habitually accustomed to rapid moves and marches, that could we be sometimes seen in our rapid and hasty movements by strangers, they would think that there was warm work in store not far in the distance. But such is not always the case, it being one of the chief features of Sherman's army; and I doubt whether a more active and energetic army has ever taken the field, or composed of better material, or accomplished more in the same length of time, as those troops under "Billy Sherman's" supervision and control. But were they to pass in review as they are seen in active raiding, through any of our large cities, they would attract unbounded attention, not in consequence of their trim appearance, but from their peculiar style; for the troops being under the necessity of packing their own. forage, it presents an interesting spectacle to behold. Some with pieces of hog unskinned stuck on the bayonets or barrels of their guns; some with their haversacks full of meal or flour; others with frying pans and coffee pots and kettles, either secured to their muskets or knapsacks, for although these articles of tin ware are not furnished by Uncle Sam, yet they find their way to the ranks in a variety of ways too numerous to mention. Although our army is large, all manage to secure some kind of cooking utensils, but frying pans are generally in great demand, as I have seen as high as $20 paid for one; and during our present raid from $5 to $20 was the ranging and average prices, and it is sometimes surprising to witness the unbounded liberality manifested in the exorbitant prices paid for anything they want or desire, as money, apparently, is no object with them. One company is allowed two regular detailed cooks, but in active service the boys dispense with their cooks, and each man goes on his own hook, and cooks his own grub, and form messes together of from two to four, each man having a kettle, coffee pot or frying pan, to suit their purpose. In consequence, it is surprising to see with what dispatch a meal's victuals is prepared at any favorable opportunity through the day; and when the boys have their full rig strapped about their persons in the form of pots, kettles, frying pans, forage, &c., they presented a unique and interesting exterior, and looked like persons well prepared for some Eldorado in the far off distance. To-day we make remarkably good time, and pass over a very good country—unusually well improved with tasty mansions and architectural beauty, and gardens ingeniously and tastefully laid out. During the afternoon, while stopping for a short time near a deserted homestead, numerous files of old papers are ferreted out, and being scattered through the ranks, are read with avidity, and a stranger would think that some extensive news depot was near at hand, or that a large mail had recently arrived; but the idea of being treated to a feast of reading matter is out of the question, as the necessity of timely reaching our distant camps is of more importance; and the day being warm, and the boys beginning to feel the effects of the day's toil, care not how soon they are allowed to hail the favored spot; however at the early hour of 4 P. M. we turned in to the right side of the road on an extensive grassy plot of land, established the boundary of our night's enclosure, and camped about one mile from Cameron Station, on the left hand side of the railroad—having marched sixteen miles. It was not long after reaching camp before the peculiar music of the swine tribe, in various directions, openly informed us of several cases of assault and battery, with intent to kill and take life, and ere fifteen minutes had ceased its vibrations, the army poachers can be seen returning with the carcasses of the slain slung on their shoulders. Being thus bountifully supplied with fresh meat in marketable condition for the army, and forgetting the laborious trials of the day, they whet their appetites for what is in store, and liberally partake of what the Confederacy has provided—squatting around nature's table in true and genuine Chinaman style.

To-day there was some cannonading to our left—the left wing of our army having met with opposition by the Johnnies, who, for the most part, have behaved uncommonly well toward the Grand Army of invasion, in our general encroachment upon their sacred soil—made sacred, at least, by the irresistible advance of an army whom nothing has yet daunted, through the center of a self-defined Confederacy, the leaders of which were but recently proud and defiant.

DEC. 5th: To-day our division takes the advance of the corps, and early day finds us at our posts, and ere twilight is succeeded by the broad glare of daylight, we are again strung out on the railroad, but before we have been long at work, imperative orders to pull out immediately reach us. The cavalry having been repulsed and driven back, we are urged forward, double quick, to their support, about seven miles in our advance. The weather being still very warm, it proves a very difficult task to keep up so rapid a pace; but after an hour or more of such rapid progress, we reach the front, where our brigade at once forms four lines of battle. In our advance we passed two lines of breastworks north of Oliver Station, near a tributary of the Ogeechee river, where a large bridge spanned the same, from which the rebels had been driven. After forming our lines of battle, we advanced some distance, when we were ordered to rest. In a short time "Uncle Billy" could be seen wending his way up to the front—for you may always rest assured that if anything is up and fighting is going to be done, he is always near by—in fact, he seems peculiarly to favor the front, and be in supporting distance with his troops at all times. He is to use familiar terms—a child of the field and front, and the idol of his command. Shortly after his arrival, and the temporary excitement being over, we were relieved from line of battle, the enemy having respectfully withdrawn, and, for the present, ceased their hostile demonstrations; and having received orders to form camp, we crossed the railroad in near proximity, from the right to the left side of same, and established our lines for the night about one mile southeast of Oliver Station, about 3 P. M., having traveled about twelve miles in all. We immediately threw out our pickets so as to be timely apprised of the near approach of the foe, should he wish to make some demonstrations on our lines during the darkness of the night, when all but the advance pickets are locked in night's soft embrace.

Dec. 6th: Having been so unceremoniously detached from our task the previous day, to attend more particularly to matters in our front, the boys cannot be expected to feel very pleasant over the announcement that we have to reverse our course and tear up the railroad track left yesterday; however, to perform this unfinished task we are aroused early and ordered to prepare for the duty. Having experienced some light showers during the silent hours of night, the morning is warm and the air bracing, and a short time subsequent to reveille, our division was swiftly gaining over the ground past yesterday, until we finally brought up the other side of the little station of Haleyondale. As we are performing our retrograde movement, we are accosted with numerous interrogatories as to our destination and the object to be achieved, which elicited numerous witty replies, such as " we are attacked in the rear," "flank movement," &c., but eventually we reached the point left yesterday, and stationing some videttes on either side of the road, the remainder go to work and vigorously prosecute the destruction of over half a mile of track, the portion allotted our regiment, when we prepared to return. During the day the whole distance, from where we commenced to far below camp, was completely destroyed by our corps. At 3½ P. M. we returned to our old camp to favor it with another night's visit, having marched about fourteen miles. Taking a common sense view of our move to-day, to a commander, one would suppose that the propriety of leaving knapsacks on such a trip as this would suggest itself at first thought, but such is the want of interest generally manifested by those in command that the boys perform much slavish and unnecessary labor for the want of sufficient interest in their welfare by those who ought to feel in duty bound to protect and see to the proper interest of those in their charge, and in consequence of this common neglect, we packed all our accoutrements, as though we were never going to return, over fourteen miles of ground to-day to a useless purpose, returning to camp toward evening, jaded out from excessive fatigue. Various instances and examples of this nature might be adduced to prove the charge, but it is not our purpose or design to deal with army failures and investigate all the wrongs of the army in these brief notes of our travel, but simply to hint the subject by the way. We have now reached that part of the state that presents another feature peculiar to the southern portion of the state, as we near the coast, in the form of moss-covered trees, hanging in

—6

graceful festoons from the wide spreading branches of live oak, decked in their winter livery of green that abound in this region.

DEC. 7th: To-day it comes our turn again to limber to the rear. During the night we experienced some heavy showers of rain, and this morning it still continues to pour down its subtle fluid, apparently unwilling to allow us a favorable opportunity to dry our shelter tents. The general appearance of things indicate slow progress and disagreeable marching in contrast with the propiteous state of things for several days past. We arose at our usual hour this morning, but ere the advance divisions were fairly under way to make room for our evacuation it was near 9 A. M.; but after a long exercise of patience we slowly moved out, taking the right side of the railroad. During the morning we make slow headway on account of bad roads caused by steady rain, and as we halt, should a patch of turnips or anything green exhibit itself, it is amusing to see the rush for the same, and in a few minutes the lot is entirely cleared of all it contained. It is surprising to see with what eagerness and avidity everything is devoured in the shape of vegetables of whatever kind, and as we are often marching along it would seem as though it was an impossibility to prevent them from leaving the ranks to go in pursuit of it when once seen. The introduction of a lot of sheep could not more completely clear the patch of its contents, and this morning, coming in contact with some of those fortunate provisional gardens, the boys make good use of what they furnish for sanitary purposes, and as we sometimes stop, there is a general huddling around some cotton press that has been previously set on fire in order to draw the dampness from the clothes and set the blood in free circulation.

One practice I must here notice that has characterized our whole raid through the State thus far, and that is, that Georgia has lost heavy in the matter of cotton, one of her staple productions. For I have been informed from good authority, that there was a special detail from each corps, mounted, whose special business it was to ferret out King Cotton for the purpose of destruction; at the same time setting fire to all the cotton houses, gins and presses found on either side of the line of march. In consequence, the sight of a burning cotton gin or cotton press, was a very common occurrence, and was one of the principal beacons to indicate our whereabouts and line of direction travelled. In fact, as King Cotton formerly claimed supremacy, the boys seemed anxious to decry its fall, and gloried in the prospect of its destruction, as they daily saw its presses and gins wrapt in glowing flames. And many a blanket and shelter tent, as well as the persons of soldiers, have been dried by the wayside by those Southern bonfires during the many disagreeable hours of slow marching caused by those drenching showers that sometime pour down in this latitude. But these were not all that was consumed, for every uninhabited house or mansion whose fugitive owners, from the stings of a guilty conscience had fled at our approach, shared the same fate, while those that remained in their domiciles, found that they largely profited by their wisdom. And it was no small number of dwellings that paid the penalty of desertion for their proprietors; and taking the general conflagrations in total, embraced in the destruction of fences, barns, corn cribs, dwellings and cotton gins and presses, it will take years of hard labor and toil, and require an immense amount of capital to replace those former evidences of industry and wealth.

But the most serious aspect of affairs within the borders of rebellion, that stares the intelligent observer in the face, is the large number of widows and orphans that are left within the blighted pale of desolation, with gaunt famine staring them in the face; and adding to this all the horrid reccollections of the past, as they are forced upon their sorrowful minds. As these terrible pictures of treason vividly portray the result of the actions of those whom they once held near and dear to them, they must produce the most galling compunctions of heart and mind; and the dawn of peace most devoutly to be wished and desired, must be a precious boon to the numerous innocent sufferers that are found scattered in the midst of those that laid their willing hands on the throat of freedom, with the intention to sap its life blood, and by the committal of this enormous crime, have brought on themselves and the innocent in their midst, the most appalling state of things.

But to return, about dusk after several hours of slow marching, we stumbled upon one of our usual swamps, the whole train being brought to a halt to allow the pioneers to repair the road for their passage. We stacked arms in an open field to the right of the road, and prepared our suppers, having up to this time made only eight miles, and receiving timely orders to prepare supper, we have concluded that there is some night work in store for us, and it literally proved true, it turning out a more severe task than we felt we had bargained for. But not being in the habit of allowing small obstacles to impede our progress, or compel us to back out, we nerved ourselves for what was in store. Shortly after our meal had been disposed of, we rusumed our journey and undertook the task of navigating our frail barks across an extensive morass in near proximity, supposing we would then meet with no further impediments to a rapid advance. But subsequent experience taught us the contrary; and instead of finding a smooth and favorable pathway to our desired haven, we experienced a continuous and uninterrupted chain of swamps and morasses, together with some pretty large flat sheets of water, in attendance.

For some time the troops studiously endeavored to avoid wading, to prevent wetting their feet, by confining themselves to those narrow foot bridges by the road side, which consist of narrow square logs having stilts firmly set in the ground, upon which they rest for a base. They succeeded for some time in their object, but some of the foot logs having been removed by some ruthless hand, the boys were finally necessitated to come down from their elevated position and try the realities of a night bath, by plunging into the watery element. No further fears are entertained, and come what may, water deep or shallow, mud deep or miry, quagmires or quicksands, roots or stumps, alligators or what not, they heedlessly pushed their way through these well watered but not very attractive regions, peculiar to this special latitude. Previous to the necessity of wading, while in the act of crossing those elevated pathways previously alluded to, many of the boys from accident or otherwise, would stumble and fall into some of those dark cesspools of corruption and stagnant pools of water, going through not a very pleasant baptismal process of introduction, and enjoying in the same meantime, a favorable opportunity of testing the hydropathic system of treatment. I sometimes fear the hydropathic system will not meet with much favor among the boys, from the frequent and unfavorable circumstances of its introduction, and during that season of the year most disagreeable. But it is hard to determine which of the three systems of practice in use, will met with the warmest support of the troops in the future. The boys have had a great opportunity of testing the practice of alipathy for the past four years, but the frequent and enormous doses of quinine, powders and pills administered to the numerous daily applicants, for various imaginary ailments and diseases, together with the immense doses of castor oil, have created such a dislike and disgust for the remedial medical agencies of this time-honored system of practice, that there may possibly exist an undue amount of prejudice against its profession and practice.

In reference to the system of hydropathy, I am inclined to think that while the boys are sometimes fond of laving the body at favorable seasons, after going through an unusual steaming process, the result of traveling at what the boys call "lightning speed," yet they are not sufficiently amphibions in their nature and taste to resort very frequently to the aqueous element, in all the numerous forms of hydropathic application. But in the system of homeopathy, they acknowledge its use pleasant, simple and easy of digestion; but the apparent childish simplicity of the practice, causes it to lose all its charms to them, if any charms there can be in its practice, treatment or results.

Returning to our journey, I would assure the reader that it was intensely disagreeable, laborious and difficult to accomplish; but the constant and uninterrupted music of the occasion, caused by the ringing screams of the boys, the sharp crackling whips of the teamsters, and the urgent appeals to the discouraged mules placed under their charge, as they earnestly endeavored to prompt them to more energetic action, in order to extricate those unwieldy army wagons as they deeply sunk in those quicksand or india rubber bottoms, strongly enlivened the occasion and acted as a spur to the moment. And whenever or wherever you hear prolonged screams, yells or roar of laughter in the front, you are apprised of unmistakable evidence of what is in store in the form of some ghastly swamp, or impassible mud hole, elicting the quaint and general exclamation, "No bottom! No bottom! Six feet! Quarter twain! Half twain! Quarter less twain!" and several others, thus imitating the log heavers on our river steamboats. After several hours of difficult night explorations through these dreaded and gloomy shades in a continuous line of swamps of about five miles in length, we emerged from those uncomfortable forest depths and went into camp not far distant, in the dark and gloomy shades of a dismal forest of lonely pines, about 1 P. M., the advance of the corps having reached the same, several hours previous; and you may rest assured that we were an unsightly looking set of mortals; for after passing the most watery portion of this inferior district previous to reaching camp, we more especially experienced a slimy strip of road that completely besmeared almost our entire persons with its well mixed contents caused by the previous passage of the advance trains. So building our camp fires with such wood as was within reach, and wringing an unusual amount of water from our drawers, pants and socks, we surrounded our sooty pine fires for want of better, and tried the application of heat to restore a healthy and proper equilibrium of things, and having performed our nightly task, the near approach of morning warned us of the necessity of a little rest, and with our scanty wardrobe of military provision, we spread our blankets on nature's couch, and the boys folding themselves between the folds of their simple arrangement, take a brief snooze ere the introduction of twilight snaps them from their much needed slumbers. To-day the advance met with some opposition, but not of a serious nature.

Dec. 8: Morning smiled propitiously on us after our previous severe treatment, and we hailed with delight it pleasant appearance, and became more reconciled to to the real state of things. For, like a son or daughter that has been chastised by the parents for breaches made contrary to parental regulation, on the exhibition of the former bland smile of true and genuine affection, the chastisement is recognised as the result of a jealous watchguard over their mien, manners and actions. So the troops sometimes are inclined to feel bitter toward high officials, who they think do not sufficiently attend to their interest during such a crucible of trial as that passed through yesterday, on the return of bright prospects, and a more genial aspect of affairs, forget the harrowing and gloomy scenes of the past, and letting it swiftly drift down oblivion's hidden channel into the forgotton past, put on a more cheerful garb, and beautifully reflect the better part of their natures in a countenance at once radiant with hope and cheerful in prospect. About 5 A. M. we arose, after a short repose of about three hours, and not being fortunate enough to close up on the advance division, we are necessitated to continue in the rear of the corps, but our brigade—centre brigade—in the division, and one regiment right center of the brigade. So after the usual paraphernalia of preparation, about 8 A. M. we again resume our journey and string out in line on the destined course of our war path. But only a short distance is left in our rear before we stumble upon one of our unwelcome obstructions, but daily visits to these unsightly monsters of the pine regions, has inured us to the difficulties attendant upon their passage. But soon bidding it a lasting farewell by widening the distance that separated us, and the morning being favorable and pleasant, we push on, being guided by the corps marks of the advance war trail. But shortly after noon we crossed at Marlow's Statien, No. 2½. It contains a neat little station house, together with some very respectable cottages, but was so small that it was scarcely worth the name of village. Having crossed to the left side of the railroad, and the enemy being disposed to dispute our advance by placing themselves in our pathway, and being in the rear, we make slow progress, while the front of our corps is treating with the rebellious Johnnies, who seem inclined to be insolent and refractory as we near the city of Savannah, made classic by the mortal remains of Baron Pulaski, who fell a martyr to the cause of liberty in the contest for independence and nationality. During the afternoon we made only two miles, when we stopped for supper by the wayside about dark, while the trains in our front were being cleared out of the way. After partaking of a very scanty meal—forage having been very scarce for the last two or three days—we grope our way along through a very flat, spongy bottom, most of the way of which had to be corduroyed. To those unacquainted with the nature of such a road, it may not be amiss to give a brief sketch of the same. In the first place, it is necessary to prevent those bulky army wagons from sinking so deeply in the mud that they cannot be extricated, as it would seriously stop and arrest the progress of the whole army train, and it being an impossibility to get plank or spare time to make a plank road, as sometimes miles have to be made during a single day. Then when we come in contact with such a road as previously described, sometimes a brigade, and at others, the whole divisions, as well as the Pioneer Corps, are regularly deployed, according to the length of each regiment. This being done, each and every man starts in pursuit of rail fences for rails, and on their return they deposit them across the road, sometimes one, two, or three deep, according to the necessity of the case. When rails cannot be secured, young trees are cut down to take their place, and if any are inclined to think this an easy road for transportation, they have only to test the matter in order to be convinced to the contrary; and such is the demand for rails during wet and disagreeable seasons, for this purpose, that every rail is used up as far as the eye can see. After passing over about four miles of this peculiar spongy bottom, we went into camp on the left hand side of the road, about 9 P. M., having traveled about thirteen miles in all. Our camp laying near Eden Station No. 2, but being rather unfortunate in our slow progress, we still camped in the rear of the 3d and 4th divisions. When, after reaching camp, the "Bummers" (as they are termed by the rank and file) can be seen returning in straggling numbers to the several camps where they belong. Many who read this may not understand the definition of the peculiar term, as it is of very recent origin, and is of purely military extraction, and will, in all probability, find a place in our vocabulary in the future. I will therefore attempt a brief description of those characters and their profession and practice. "Bummers" most generally belong to that peculiar class termed by the rank and file "Pimps," that are commonly found in such large numbers at the numerous headquarters—from the chief general's commanding down to regimental. Although they all belong to some regiment or the other embraced in the department, but to this particular class of individuals active service is not congenial or agreeable to their notion of things, and in consequence they much prefer to fill the numerous positions that have to be filled by somebody, in preference to active service in the ranks. Filling those positions they can more easily secure the requisite passports, so as to branch out on either flank for forage or what not. Once clear of the main line of travel, and out of the sight and reach of the guards, they commence to develop their plundering and pilfering propensities on a scale commensurate with their wants, and you can depend on the fact that but little escapes their detection, and the more securely anything is placed under lock and key, the more determined they are to sound its contents. The variety of eatables found, whether in large or small supplies, is not what they are always strictly after, and should they not succeed, after a thorough search through every nook and corner of the house, and the breaking open of everything under lock and key, they then threaten violence to the half affrighted negroes if they do not make known the place of its concealment; and firmly believing their threats will be carried into execution, they develop the place of its secret deposit, which the eager and avaricious bummer at once secures. The articles mostly wanted by them consists of gold and silver, watches and jewelry, and gold and silver ware, or plated, as the case may be, together with a variety of other articles too numerous to mention. Previous to their return at night, they bring in the necessary amount of forage for the officers for whom they forage, and for the benefit of the messes to which they belong—which generally consists of the best to be secured. A large percentage of the "bummers" is also furnished from the trains and hangers-on around the same—as they generally keep a good supply of mules, and can more conveniently carry the results of their plunder, not having to pack their knapsacks. It is astonishing, and sometimes amusing, to see the various tricks resorted to for the success of their enterprise, but the negroes are the ones upon whom they try their skill with wonderful success, for in their peculiar natural cunning, they most commonly succeed in finding where their masters secret their treasures, and the boys knowing the nature of their dupes, easily compel them by threats to reveal the mysterious secret. Others, by holding a rod in their hand, similar to the practice of water witches, who claimed to be able to decide where to succeed in securing water by the peculiar dip of the rod at the spot where such is to be found, and by this simple practice they make the untutored negroes believe; they divine, by these means, the place of all concealed valuables, and the negroes, thinking they are possessed of witchery, hastily volunteer to divulge its whereabouts. But some are more bold and daring, and unceremoniously entering the house, they rifle it from top to bottom, and in the non-success of what they are in search of, numerous vociferations is the result, and to show to what extent these "bummers" sometimes carry their projects, I will relate a single instance. A matronly lady hearing that her provisions would be taken from her at the approach of our army, had secreted them between the folds of her bed, and to better secure and prevent their escape—assumed the attitude of a convalescent, and reposed her delicate frame on the virtuous couch, not harboring the least suspicion that her person would be molested in that innocent and confiding position. After a while a number of "bummers" came rushing up in hot haste, each anxious to precede the other, and abruptly introduced themselves to an inside view of the humble mansion. The peculiar order of things was soon made manifest to their senses, and in their usual manner at once commenced an unceremonious and hasty search, but not succeeding according to their expectations, they bethought themselves that they might succeed in finding objects of their search in the folds of the bed whereon the lady reclined ; and banishing all modest pretensions, they announced to the now blushing matron that they were under the necessity of disturbing her rest, as they wished to ascertain the contents of such a mammoth couch, and to her great chagrin, they found an abundance of good things, of which the bed was at once relieved, and the wit and cunning of the good lady completely thwarted. But this is only one of the many occurrences of like nature that might be adduced to prove the unhallowed calling of those army poachers, and these "bummers" succeeding well in finding the hidden treasures of the South, well know that nearly every house and family have recourse to the same practice to prevent the loss of what is near and dear to them, and with this knowledge, when not succeeding within the dwelling, they charge the owners with this guilt, and by their threats they generally succeed in making the negroes divulge its whereabouts, and in consequence, most of the hidden treasures are secured.

I am well satisfied that the citizens of the South will acknowledge an almost impossibility to hide, or place anything beyond the reach of the ingenious Yankee ; and it would be surprising to know the vast amount of stuff hidden in the woods and swamps, as well as horses, mules, &c., &c., in our raid through the State, which was captured by that class in search of the same ; but it was in our raid through the Carolinas, that this peculiar profession met with such unbounded success ; and should any wish to discover the "Bummer's trail," they had only to branch out on either side of the road, when they could discover that the woods were completely ramified with the same, and whenever the troops discovered paths diverging from our main line of march, they at once recognized and designated them as the "Bummer's trail." But they are not always safe to follow as they sometimes lead through swamps, bogs and quagmires not very easy to navigate. Another feature practiced by those who aim to be successful in this profession is, to change their general appearance by doffing their dress of blue, and garbing themselves in butternut style, with an old "plug hat," to complete their full equipment ; and then with the air of a southerner they ply their profession in genuine guerilla style, but the numerous tricks and make-shifts resorted to by these army gents, I have not time to enumerate, and is not my present object ; and believing that professional writers will do the subject more justice than I have time to do in this brief sketch, I will proceed with the narration of our march.

The night was delightfully pleasant and the silvery queen of night shone with unusual brilliancy upon us, beautifully lighting up our entire camp, while the commissary issued a scanty supply of hard tack and coffee to us, these being the only articles of supply in the train, and but little of those. Our camp being rather narrow and contracted in its limits, the different regiments of the division are huddled together unusually close, and after our usual preliminary preparations, we bid a good and pleasant night to all, except those whom we know would willingly disturb our rest, could they conveniently accomplish it.

DEC. 9th: Having to take the front to-day, we are not allowed to doze very late in the morning in harmless silence, but at the stated hour of 4 o'clock A. M., all are apprised of needed action; and having to pass two divisions, third and fourth, not much ceremony is observed in our customary morning duties; and shortly after the break of day, we commenced to move out in a style that usually betrayed the nature of the task that followed. Talleyrand says, " A man's reputation is like his shadow, gigantic when it precedes him, but pigmy in its proportions when it follows after." So our task generally turns out to be gigantic when we experience its previous indications.

To-day the 3d brigade was in the advance; 1st in the rear, 2d in the center. After pulling out on the road, we marched nearly on the double-quick, a distance of about seven miles, passing the third and fourth divisions on the road. The morning was cloudy and cool, and we could already distinguish the bracing effects of a sea breeze, the wind blowing from the coast, which somewhat favored our rapid marching. About seven miles from camp we battled against the Johnnies, which somewhat raised their ire, and put their combative propensities in full exercise; and our division being pitted against them under the dashing leadership of Major General Mower, it now becomes us to decide whether we shall be bluffed by the Johnnies in our advance by their hostile demonstrations or not. The fourth division in the advance, dealt with them yesterday and compelled their retirement, and we are to demonstrate its practical utility to-day. For this purpose, the 32nd Wisconsin of the third brigade, is deployed on the skirmish line on the right, while the remainder of the division, with the exception of two companies, advanced in lines of battle. Companies B and G, of our regiment, was deployed out as line of skirmishers on the left flank, and the first Alabama cavalry still to the left of us. The disposition of the troops being fully arranged, we steadily compel them to give way before us, a distance of seven miles, sharp skirmishing going on the whole distance. The rebels used a battery on us with some effect and damage, but did not materially hinder our progress; we also had to effect the passage of some ugly swamps in our advance, which was not very comforting to us in our otherwise warm circumstances. During the day, the 32nd Wisconsin and 35th New Jersey, had several killed and wounded, and several were killed and wounded by torpedoes in the division; and taking some prisoners, we compelled them to point out their whereabouts, and extract them from their hiding places, which they did not well relish. Our division quartermaster, Captain Hamrick, was also killed by a piece of a shell, and some torpedo accidents occurred in the Alabama cavalry. In fact, the task of advancing was not a very pleasant or cool one, and the aggregate of the day's damage was considerable through the division.

Half past two o'clock, P. M., found us fourteen miles from the last encampment, and the rebels having retreated a respectful distance, we established our camp for the night, and during the afternoon and early part of the evening, we threw up a line of works as a cautionary measure, to prevent a surprise, and to be fully prepared should they be disposed to give us a trial of their skill and strength. The afternoon was very chilly, accompanied with a drizzling, misty rain, which from the effects of our swamp wading, made it very disagreeable. Our foraging, having in military phraseology, "played out," and the supply of rations in haversacks, being scanty—especially meat—the boys can be seen ransacking and scouring the woods in quest of live stock, of whatever kind they can find. The work of securing it is a more difficult enterprise than some imagine, as shooting is expressly forbidden and prohibited, sometimes under a severe penalty. This being the case, the boys resort to various methods for success, one of which was resorted to this afternoon. Having a very wild and untractable heifer to secure, they surrounded it, and gradually narrowing the circle down to a small diameter, they make a plunge for its tail, which often turns out, not a very safe undertaking. One of the number having secured it, clings to it with all the muscular strength he has to spare ; the heifer in the meantime making desperate plunges to extricate herself; but others jumping, in, secure the same hold, and pull in an opposite direction with all their might having by these means considerably retarded her progress ; another jumped in and secured her by the horns, while the executioner with the axe, struck the fatal blow; but it often turns out that the adventurers get a little worsted, and can be seen sprawling on the ground in near proximity, while the poor animals make good their retreat, to elude if possible, further pursuit. A novel method of securing hogs is effected by surrounding them, and when they undertake to break the charmed circle, by storming the works, in passing the one they seek to elude, he throws himself with wonderful dexterity upon his victim, endeavoring if possible, to secure a firm grasp, either on the ears, tail, or legs, in which he often succeeds, while another dispatches him with the weapon in waiting. But sometimes the hog gets the better of his adversary and drags him along on the ground for some distance, and at other times, turns upon his captor in the contest for supremacy. And I have even seen some of the more desperate of our army, while the swine were in hot and hasty retreat, throw themselves with daring ingenuity and activity, across the backs of the animals, and instantly grabbing a hold on the ears of their antagonists would maintain their positions in horseback style, until others had performed the crowning tragedy of the act, although they would have to maintain their positions some distance before its final accomplishment. But these are only a few of the various contrivances they have recourse to, for a liberal supply of animal food, when short of rations and nothing else can be had ; and the wonderful dispatch with which it is all done, would astonish many of our city butchers, who make it their profession and practice. Sometimes within fifteen minutes from the time of life, they are stewing in the pan, and transferred from the field of life to the purposes of the kitchen. This is not done and put up in a very marketable condition for city purchasers, but very well answers the purposes of the troops, when their larders are scantily furnished, and the commissary well nigh emptied of its contents. Having satisfied the present demands of the appetite, all further trouble is soon forgotten, and it is a well known fact in army experience, that if present demands are satisfied, but little care is borrowed for the future, as it is sufficient for them that the

—7

present wants are supplied, they let the future provide for itself. So after the particulars and results of the day's excitement have been fully canvassed and talked over, and its most dangerous incidents pointed out, and its success and final issue arrived at, they conclude it enough for one day's compendium. And having arrived at the final conclusion—that there is warm work in store for the morrow—they can be seen busily preparing for a warm seclusion from the chilling effects of a cold wind, and are soon cosily wrapped in their blankets, forgetful of the exciting scenes of the past day.

CHAPTER VI.

THE SIEGE OF SAVANNAH AND THE ALTAMAHA RAID.

Commencement of the Siege—Encircling the City—An Artillery Duel—Heavy Skirmishing on the Left—An Effort to close up on the Left of the 15th Corps—Hunger Staring us in the Face—Army Beef—A Move to the Right—Chuck-a-luck Banks—Their Tendency—Intense Suffering from Cold—Negro Adventure—Trial of Hydropathic Treatment—A General Performance—Capture of Fort McAllister and its Results—Communication with the Fleet—Description of a Camp—Hard Living—Food Commanding High Prices—Trip to the Ogeechee—First Arrival of Mail—Its Electrifying Influence—Raid to the Altamaha—Midway Church and Cemetery—Ladies Private Correspondence—Success of the Enterprise—Rapid Marching—The Welcome Issue of Hard Tack—Return to Camp—Evacuation of the City—Our Possession—Everything Left in Our Hands—20th Corps Garrison the City—Army Camped in near Proximity—Johnnies Tired of the Cause—Dressed in Ladies Attire to Escape the Service—Important Captures.

DEC. 10th: During the previous night our camp lay in position near Pooler Station, about nine miles from the city. The morning was cloudy and lowering, and gave intimations of an uncomfortable day. But should there be warm work in store for us the weather would prove very exhilerating and favorable for the necessary action. We were stirred from our slumbers at 5 A. M., and at seven o'clock we could be seen vacating our last encampment in order to a closer approximation to the city. Our course was on one of the main pikes to the city, on a parallel line with the railroad. But we were not permitted to travel over four and a half miles towards the city, ere the iron monsters came shrieking through the atmosphere, scattering their ponderous and deadly contents through the lines and among the trains, warning us of the danger consequent to our further advance. "Uncle Billy" could be seen as usual under the exciting condition of affairs close up to the front, and it was at this particular juncture of affairs, that he barely escaped contact with a deadly cannon ball, and at the same time it missed him, it produced quite a scattering among the trains. As the shells were beginning to tell with terrible effect, seven being killed and some wounded by a single shell, this necessitating prompt action on our part, Gen. Mower could be seen busily reconnoitering the general situation, in order to make a proper disposition of his command. The second brigade being in advance, it furnished the requisite number of troops for the skirmish line, our brigade forming at once in line of battle, the third being kept in reserve. A short time developed the necessary disposition of troops, and we commenced at once to move to the right, a favorable position being selected for the planting of a battery. The Third Michigan, Battery C, came up willing and ready as usual to try their general aptitude and skill, as they had often done before during the Atlanta campaign of the summer months, with terrible effect, while our brigade lay near by within supporting distance. The Fourth Division of our corps joined us on the left, and we united with the 15th Corps on our right, while the Third Divison lay near by in our rear. About this time we changed our position, going still further to the right, and crossed the Ogeehee canal at this place, part of our division having previously plunged in and waded the same, crossing over to the other side, and established a skirmish line across a field between the canal and a large swamp, another impassible swamp lying between the skirmish line and the rebel works. Having crossed the canal we lay under shelter of a high bank near the margin of the canal, while the Third Battery, previously spoken of, did some terrible execution to the rebels, they for sometime promptly replying to our calls until near night, when the rebel artillery ceased its firing. During the progress of the artillery duel, the commanding general-in-chief paid a visit to this particular part of the line, attended only by a single staff officer, and dismounted under the bank, leaving his horse in charge of a member of the company to which I belong. He proceeded on foot to reconnoiter the position of the rebel lines, and on his return appeared well pleased at the favorable aspect of affairs. Gen. Blair and staff also greatly exposed themselves at the same time, to find out, and select the most favorable positions to operate from, and both, I was informed, received pretty close calls in their hazardous undertaking. Maj. Gen. Mower was not behind the foremost in the difficult and dangerous enterprise, losing one of his staff officers, Lieut. O'Rielly, in the operation. Toward night our brigade relieved part of the second, they moving off more to our left to give us room. Our regiment advanced across the open field on the margin of a large swamp, and deployed in line of skirmishers, and as I was informed for the purpose of advancing the line over the swamp in our front.

After remaining some time in anxious expectation of further commands, we received orders again to move back over the rising ground to the edge of the woods in our rear. In this operation we met with no serious opposition from our wily antagonists, and having digested our suppers, we secured a sufficient number of rails to build a line of works, which during the night we accomplished, on the highest part of the rising ground previously spoken of. Thus during the silent hours of the night, the city was partly encircled with a belt of works that bade defiance to the rebel foe in our front; and from this time began the brief period of its seige, which ultimately resulted in its occupation by the loyal besiegers. The night was very cold, and after the completion of our line of works, we sheltered ourselves as best we could from its inclemency. The rebels during the mean time behaved very civil, as they did not molest us, but rather allowed us to proceed in peace and quietness with our task.

A few brief hours of rest, ushored in the morning of the 10th, and in taking a view of the state of affairs in our front, we discovered in full view a very formidable fort and other substantial works, which well accounted for their civility during the night, and seemingly well prepared for the harsh treatment they anticipated was in store for them. The white appearance of the works seemed to indicate a free and liberal use of King Cotton in their construction, and as the light of day dawn with more clearness on our visions, we could see them still busily engaged in their erection and completion. It was not long before our battery opened on them vigorously with skill and execution, and considerably battered down and levelled each side of the embrasures of their forts, until we completely silenced and prevented them from replying, and the works that this morning looked frowning and formidable to our situation, were, about noon, considerably dilapidated. Their shells and rifle bullets did not do much execution on our lines, as we compelled them to lie close, and in consequence, not many casualties occurred in our division, only one being wounded in Co. B of our regiment, and a few accidents in nearly every other regiment in the division, but the aggregate number was not large.

While the cannonading was going on, the pioneer corps was testing the possibility of constructing a pathway across the terrible swamp that separated the right of our division (the 3d brigade) from the left of the 15th corps. A detail as advanced skirmishers being furnished by our regiment to precede the pioneers while they faithfully endeavored to erect a pathway. After working several hours at the difficult task in their advance, until the skirmishers were up to their arm pits in water, and also the pioneers, till their teeth chattered from the chilling effect of the cold water and the atmosphere, the project was abandoned and considered next to impossible to accomplish, the boys being well satisfied to abandon such a disgusting and disheartening undertaking, were not slow in making good their exit from such a dismal obstruction to our present success. During the day constant and rapid skirmishing was going on at the left of the 15th corps, but during the afternoon it was more quiet on our portion of the line, which ran thus—3d brigade on the right, 2d brigade on the left, and ours in the center, and the right of the 4th division on our left. About 4 P. M., the 4th division as well as ours was relieved by the 14th corps, we at the same time withdrawing, moved out from the line, resumed our course, travelled toward the right some four or five miles, when we camped for the night. It was intensely cold for this climate, and the wind blowing a perfect hurricane, the boys being short of clothes suffered much, and were glad to take shelter beneath the folds of their blankets.

During the time occupied by our division in the part played by them in commencing the siege of Savannah, the 10th Illinois, 32d Wisconsin and 35th New Jersey, sustained the greatest loss, and the 53d Illinois of the 4th division, lost heavy—one company having about ten killed and wounded by a single shell. But every regiment acted well its part, and went wherever it was bidden, and it was necessary that short work should be made in our contest for the possession of the city, as we had previously used up all the hard tack that was in the supply train, coffee being the only article of army rations in the train left for issue. Our haversacks of emptiness already stared us in the face, and foraging having previously played out, we were reduced to the direful necessity of accepting and subsisting on army beef and unhulled rice, these being the only articles of provisions within the power of the commissary to furnish, until such times as we could clear away the formidable obstructions that prevented their arrival. And to those unexperienced in the difficult mastication of army beef, it would well repay a fair trial. I am satisfied they would acknowledge it a dear bargain, to bestow upon it the labor necessary to prepare it for digestion, and acknowledge that they never knew the use of poor beef up to such a time. For, be it understood, that by the time they have been driven on foot from the Ohio river to the coast, at all hours and under all circumstances, by night and by day, through streams, swamps, bogs, quagmires, woods, and dense bush, with scarcely anything to eat but what they could pick up by the way, and huddled together in big droves and placed in all conceivable circumstances, that by the time it is issued to the rank and file, most of the flesh has disappeared from the bones, leaving nothing but the frame work or structure to be issued to the troops—the very smell of it sometimes proving very disagreeable to one's olfactories. Woe to the man under such circumstances as the present, who is wanting in those indispensable organs of mastication; he would surely learn to appreciate their real value, and suffer much from their untimely absence. In fact, you have need to put it through a twenty-four hours boiling process, ere it is fit for an introduction to the stomach, or your rest will be considerably encroached upon. Many of those walking skeletons often drop down and die by the wayside, for the want of sufficient strength to prosecute their further journey, and hundreds in this poor, weak and shattered condition, are slaughtered for the army. This is the kind of animal food palmed off on the troops at times when they most need what is calculated to nourish and strengthen, to maintain life.

In reference to unhulled rice, the boys were for a time totally at a loss to know what disposition to make of it, and not having machinery to separate the hulls from the rice, they would resort to various expedients and contrivances to insure success, in which at the best, we could only partially be successful, and proving very unpalatable in this respect. Sometimes the boys would use the wooden pestle and mortar very much in vogue among the negroes for hulling their own stated allowances of the same. For this purpose, all those particular articles of manufacture in the surrounding neighborhoods, were gathered up and put in active use. They very much resemble the apothecaries pestle and mortar, only the cavity of the mortar is more pointed and the pestle framed perfectly in accordance. They are very bulky and weighty, and require a great expenditure of muscular power to make much headway in the operation. But grub is in great demand, and hungry stomachs calling for satisfaction, its operation is rendered a military necessity, and the boys in the numerous regiments could be seen working with a will to satisfy a ravenous appetite created by a cold bracing atmosphere that had taken possession of the "Sunny South" at this critical and important juncture. But to return, the critical position of the 4th division, rendered it very unsafe for them to move out until night had set in and mantled the scene with her sombre curtain, and during the late hours of evening they silently withdrew, and moving a respectful distance on the same line of road with us, they established their camp for the night.

DEC. 12th. This morning the cold was more intense than last evening, and the lateness of the hour of our arrival in camp prevented us from pitching our tents, and receiving early intimation to arise, we emerged from our blankets to find that "Mr. Jack Frost" had paid us an unwelcome visit, and left his icy marks behind to be testimony to the same. It was as early as 4 A. M. that our rest was broken in upon, and the cold and piercing wind rolling in violence through the scattering pines, as we once more endeavored to place ourselves erect on terre firma, made the cold chills to be felt keenly through our whole systems, as we were short of the clothing necessary to be warm during the presence of such an untimely visitor, and what we had was becoming threadbare, and showed visible marks of hard usage. Rails being scarce, and but little dry wood near at hand, there was a guard huddling around the fires of those that had been fortunate enough to secure fuel, and as the wind would hurl its frosty contents against the boys with its extreme violence, they could be seen vainly endeavoring to contract their dimensions, and coil up from its piercing stings in order to avoid its smarting effects. Overcoats are a luxury, and it would seem as though we were unjustly punished for the want of them; for at one time the "Lord of Day" punishes us, it would seem, for being overloaded with dry goods, and at another "Mr. Frost," for not having sufficient. Thus were we goaded between two extremes—scarcely knowing which of the two punishments to decide in favor of—blaming one for being too cold, the other for being too warm, causing perpetual strife between us and the elements, and sometimes accusing both of being bent on our destruction. At 7½ A. M. we were all in readiness to move. Our quarters affording us but slight accommodations, and our treatment anything but friendly, we cared not how soon we were on the way, so as to assist or accelerate the sluggish circulation of the vital fluid. A short distance brought us on the pike we left two days previous, and traveling two miles on the same evening, turned off to the left on a very narrow road, so as to circle around the large swamp, previously mentioned, to the right, and being swampy or marshy on either side. The troops and train have to occupy the same, thereby causing the army to be unduly strung out. Each division train follows in the rear of its own division, and each division commander has charge of his own division train, and is under the necessity of attending to its due and proper advancement, and each brigade and regiment takes its proper turn as guard to the same, and to assist it over those difficult and miry spots that we oftimes come in contact with. Consequently it is a great help to the progress of an army from what it was when under the supervision of one man, causing miles of train to be blocked on the road at one time, without a proper distribution of troops to prepare the way for its timely advance; and by such an incomplete organization, greatly hinder an army's progress. Each division train takes the ordnance, quartermaster, and commissary stores for its own division; in fact, all the necessary articles needed simply for active campaigning. The roads being narrow, and the country very flat, and the army thereby unduly strung out, we progressed very slowly, and being very cold, it is exceedingly disagreeable; nevertheless, at every hault of any length, the "Chuck-a-luck banks" can be seen in active operation in different parts of the regiments—many of the army seem apparently to be fed and kept up on excitement—and numbers could be seen staking their all on the last throw, win or loose, and many an unsuspecting mind, on their early introduction to military life, has been warily drawn into this whirling mælstrom of destruction, and transformed from a youth of promising appearance to a giddy, whirling, dissipated wreck of humanity. It is astonishing to see its general prevalence in our army, owing to the absence of parental instruction, and the wise counsel and sympathy of those who know the demon shades of its practice, and the dark abodes of its leading votaries; for let once its poisonous fangs pierce the soul, and it would seem as though the last ray of glimmering hope is extinguished, and, like the "Worm of the Still," it every day fastens its hold more securely on its victims, when, like the degraded victims and dupes of the cruel "Juggernaut," they are crushed beneath its ponderous machinery. For I have seen, after the troops have been paid off, as many as thirty banks in full blast, huddled together within a single circle, and in one short hour the last dime of eight months pay is squandered at one of these delirious stands.

As we are slowly wending our way along in those narrow defiles of our circuitous route to-day—which are all of artificial construction by the process of digging large, deep ditches on either side—much occurred to amuse and wile away the time. One old negro, whose judgment one would have supposed more correct in such matters, was jogging along, mounted on an old plug horse, somewhat worse by use, in the rear of the 39th Ohio, when the troops came to a halt, undertook to let his horse stop to drink out of those side-road ditches, when, by an extra effort, he plunged himself, rider and all his kit into this miniature canal, the whole trio becoming completely submerged by the accident, but on their appearance to the surface of the sluggish fluid, the negro still maintaining his position on the back of the animal, kept urging him to extra efforts to extricate himself from such a perilous position, at the same time pulling the reins with all of his muscular might; thus instead of accomplishing his purpose, he only sank the animal deeper in the mire at the bottom; the boys, in the meantime, were vigorously exercising their stentorian lungs in loud peals of laughter while the act was being performed; finding he could not succeed, he dismounts, placing himself once more on terra firma, dragging the lank, half starved beast after him, and thereby presenting a unique and interesting spectacle to his highly interested and excited audience. The bath was not a pleasant one, as the day was very unfavorable for hydropathic treatment, and the presence of some warm fire would prove far more exhilerating, and much more attractive under such unpleasant circumstances.

While the negro performance was being enacted, the mules in near proximity commenced some of their curious antics, and deposited their riders and pack on the ground, and thereby claimed an interest in the general glee, by performing an important part in the drama; however, mules will be mules, and soldiers will have their pastime in dramatic performances, tragic scenes and comic farces, whether or not, and amid all the hardships, toils and dangers of military life, yet their motto still is:

> "Let the wide world wag as it will,
> We'll be gay and happy still."

In the course of the day's events we again stumbled on the Ogeechee canal, and crossed the same about four miles above our line of works, where we first crossed it, although we had already made a circuit of some twelve miles. The 2nd brigade preceding us had been sent up at the head of the canal, in consequence of hearing that a force of rebels were stationed there, while the remainder of the division, after a respectable halt on the other side, made for camp, about three miles distant. Our camp lay on the left hand side of the road in the rear of the line of 15th army corps. We reached the same about half past nine, P. M., having made a circuit of fifteen miles, but on a bee line only about four, or at the most, five miles from the position previously left. Having stacked arms, there is a general pell-mell rush in every direction for rails or whatever can be secured of firewood, the boys having to travel from three-fourths to a mile and a half after them, but it was very cold, and with them wood must be had, whether far or near, and woe to the untenanted house or barn or any other building that presents itself to view under such circumstances; a few minutes will suffice to see it borne off on the backs of those in quest of it. I have seen large frame buildings in a brief space of time, disappear with scarcely a vestige left to prove that a building ever stood there, with the exception of a few brick or stone piers, or a solitary chimney, to mark the place of its site. After the necessary preparations for the morning were attended to, and rations such as they were, had been issued to us, and our own scanty suppers disposed of, it was well nigh the hour of midnight, and the boys for want of sufficient clothing to keep the body warm, concluded to bivouack for the night and try a closer contact with mother earth, beneath their simple covering, in hopes of a more congenial atmospheric treatment on the morrow.

DEC. 13th: This is the day that witnessed the grand assault and capture of Fort McAllister. At a council of war held by the Generals commanding in the department of the Tennessee, it was to be decided by a vote, which division should be awarded the task and have the honor (if such it may be called) of its capture. The first division of the 17th army corps, Major General Mower commanding, and the second division of the 15th army corps, Brigadier General Hazen commanding. The latter received a majority of two votes; the task of its accomplishment fell to their lot accordingly, on the afternoon of the 13th. Every preparation and caution was made by the brave and heroic commander to insure success, and the arrangement and disposition of his troops so ordered as to effect its capture in a brief space of time, to prevent all unnecessary bloodshed and loss of life in the momentary struggle. The line was formed about six hundred yards from the fort, and at the signal for action, the gallant charge was made, and in the brief space of five minutes the brave actors in the tragic and exciting scene, were seen scaling the mammoth works, and ere its defenders were prepared to do any terrible execution, they had secured a lodgment within its precincts, but for some time it was a hand to hand contest between the defenders and the brave assaulters; but the gallant chargers constantly pressing on all sides, they were soon overpowered, and compelled to yield to their victors, the garrison and all its equippage. The division lost in the assault 134 killed and wounded,—and took in the operation a large amount of commissary stores and liquors, 24 pieces of light and heavy ordnance, 100 stand of small arms, and 60 tons of ammunition. The enemy's loss in killed and wounded was 35, and in prisoners 195.

Thus was unlocked one of the most important obstacles necessary to effect an entrance to one of the most important cities of the coast. The following evening, Maj. Gen. Sherman established communications on board of the fleet, and dated his first dispatch to the President from Osabaw Sound, announcing the important capture of the fort, and its garrison equippage; and already considered the city of Savannah as good as in his possession. Thus was fairly demonstrated the possibility of penetrating for several hundred miles, the enemy's country and disembowelling some of their main arterial channels of circulating life, and in the brief space of 31 days from the time that we severed the electric current of loyal communication, and laid the important highway of our provisional channel, (that had supplied our penetrating army during the summer months with supplies), in a mass of ruins from beyond the Big Kenesaw down. We had established a new base and took the offered privilege of using Neptune's aid to accomplish our further conquests in the firm resolve to prostrate treason's ghastly hydra-headed form. The weather to-day sobered itself down to our convenience, and the sun shone with unusual brightness on the arena of action, as if unusually smiling at the general progress and prospect of affairs. And the boys were not more pleased with the genial warmth of Heaven's bright luminary, than with the prospective view of soon hearing again from the homes of their childhood, and the many loving ones left behind, whose cheering notes long since on the way will fill their very souls with rapturous joy and lift many a one from a state of despondency to a more cheerful view of the existing state of things. Oh! ye wives, sisters, mothers, &c.; if ye could only sometimes witness the estatic delight your àffectionate letters create, you would never neglect to send so cheap a boon to those who are doating on your affectionate breathings with almost idol worship, and watching with intense zeal its seasonable return, at the arrival of every mail. I can assure you I have sometimes seen many of those faithful sentinels on the highest battlements of the watch tower, almost delirious with joy at the safe arrival of the precious casket that contains the priceless jewel of affection and the warm breathings of genuine love. Language is altogether inadequate to describe its reviving effects, as it causes the vital fluid to bound through the different part of the previously prostrated system, restoring a healthy and joyous equilibrium throughout the whole. To-day foraging parties were sent out in quest of forage for the trains, and the remainder of the division could be seen basking in the rays of the sun, waiting for orders to move, while the remainder of our army, busily prosecuting the siege, were during the day incessantly exchanging salutes in a manner not altogether polite or decorous, and were exchanging conversation in language too plain to be misunderstood; some of which resulted in blows unceremoniously bestowed at very short notice, resulting in mutual damage to the contending parties. But the ire of both being excited, they are not easily dissuaded from giving up the contest, and the weak but aggressive party being sheltered behind their massive breastworks, seem not disposed at present to allow us a triumphal entrance, and thus place their frowning mouth-pieces in our way, and occasionally give us an intimation in thunder tones of the danger to be incurred, should we be disposed to test the dangerous barrier. As an accompaniment to the rest could distinctly be heard the crackling of musketry in its usual barking, and sometimes biting style, as it alternately played its important part in the melo-dramatic concert, being given at great expense and cost, and no pains were spared on either side to insure complete success in the several parts, by the agitated rivalry on both sides. In the afternoon, being informed of another night's lodging in this unattractive region, the troops could be seen busily engaged in pitching their tents in order to ameliorate their condition during their short pilgrimage, and shortly was presented to view the happy scene of an unwalled city in true patriarchial style, with each regimental square block, and their broadway in front on the color line, with neat little streets intersecting every company, while at a respectable distance in the rear of each regiment and company, were the line officers' quarters not differing from ours, only by being more conspicuous.

The two following days were taken up principally in breaking camp, moving quarters, preparing color line, drilling, inspections, sending out foraging parties, &c., and what time was not consumed in these particular vocations, was spent in pounding out unhulled vice, and stewing down to a passable condition for use the army beef, which we have previously noticed. These being the only articles of commissary supplies issued, and by the time we had attended to those numerous d ities, and packed our wood and water to camp, a mile distant, we were not sorry, at the close of each, to dream our troubles away in the land of forgetfulness, and enjoy a short respite from such a disgusting routine of duty. And such was the scarcity of rations at this critical date, that I have seen the boys pay as high as two dollars for from six to a dozen ears of corn to parch, money being no object with them in comparison with necessary food.

On the morning of the 16th all was on the alert, and activity and bustle per-

8—

vaded the entire camp. The troops not being fondly attached to their camp, care
not how soon they make their exit from its unpleasant association, and go in search
of a new position. About 9 A. M. we received orders to pack up, and ere long
had made one mile from camp, when the order was countermanded, and we again
returned, but we had scarcely prepared for another night's stay, when we received
orders to be ready to march at 2½ P. M.; and at the appointed time for departure,
the 1st and 3d brigades of our division pulled out, and going about one mile south
of camp, we took a direct course for the Ogeechee river, at which place we arrived
shortly after dusk, it being about four and a half miles southwest of our camp.
The point at which we camped was at the head of steamboat navigation, where a
bridge spans the stream. During the afternoon, the first steamer came up the river,
with mail, anchoring close to the bridge previously referred to. The mail was at
once landed, selected, and sent to the different army corps for distribution. During
the hours of evening, sack after sack of mail arrived at the several regiments of
our division, and was distributed to its owners. It caused intense joy and excitement amongst them, and all through the several camps they could be seen flocking
together around their dimly burning fires trying to fan the slowly burning embers
into a flame, so as to be enabled to read (what was to them) the all important news.
Numbers that previously retired for the night could be seen issuing from their
warm seclusion, to devour the mental feast in store for them. A general expression of satisfaction marked the countenances of all fortunate enough to hear of
loved ones at home, and such was the frank and open outbursts of joy and thank-
fulness, that it was long after midnight before many retired, and when they did, it
was only to think of the kind and tender expressions of sympathy that was breathed,
and that permeated every sentence of those love tokens. Mothers and sweet-
hearts, it would have done your soul good to have seen the electrifying influence
of your kind and soothing words, as they touched the tender cords of sympathy,
and made them well up from the innermost depths of the heart in their reactionary
results. You would never spare so cheap a boon and cheering a cordial when once
you experienced its successful application. It was the best medicine issued for
some time, and produced the most exhilarating effects, and although there was a
rapid march to follow in its train, it was accomplished with more ease and success
than I ever knew a march of the same nature in the same length of time. Quinine
and blue mass was in poor demand for some time afterward, and the quick, light
step betokened a light heart, as the yearning load of anxiety had been rolled off
their backs. They felt like "Bunyan's Christian," wonderfully relieved. This general good feeling can be well accounted for from the fact that the boys had received no mail from home for six weeks. In short, it was a gala day to them—
a mental harvest, a delightful wreath woven by affection's loom that was en
twined around the heart and brow of the receiver. But this is only the bright side
of the picture. To an intelligent observer, many a countenance could be seen to
wear an air of disappointment and sorrow. The long looked for information had
not arrived; its cause they could not divine; and the dark suspicious forebodings
that would loom up in all their intensity and harrass their already perplexed minds,
until their very manhood would quiver at the ghastly and frightful internal picture
of demon intrusion. Man is a social being, and loves to have an object on which to
place his affections, and however much hardened to the cruel scenes of war, the
notes of love will touch the chords of sympathy, and place them in lively exercise,

when nothing else will succeed. Prove that you are their friends and it will awaken the liveliest emotions in their breasts. But the fault in the non-reception of mail is not always at home, but in its careless handling during its passage through the numerous channels it has to pass. After the principal excitement is over, and the news well digested, general quietness again prevails, and supreme silence has trken its place, and all are enjoying a brief repose preparatory to the duties of the morrow. During the ensuing five days much was to be accomplished. Major General Mower having received orders to penetrate as far as possible to the Altamaha river, and destroy the railroad for five or six miles, on this side of the same, and, on the principle that the early bird catches the worm, we were early on the wing. Having received no rations the previous evening, and our empty haversacks staring us in the face, we all felt anxious to lay in a supply. Our appetites were already pretty keenly whetted by a previous fast; and, believing that we could do ample justice to a fair supply of "Uncle Sam's" hard tack under present circumstances, we were all wistfully looking for its appearance according to promise, but after exhausting our patience in anxious expectation of its arrival, we were under the "military necessity" of pulling out. However being subsequently informed of the cause of such treatment, the boys kept a stiff upper lip, with a determination to brave the worst. It seems that a boat had been dispatched up the river with rations for us, but from contact with torpedoes in the river, was disabled from making the trip. It was General Mower's desire to lay over until rations could be brought from Fort McAllister, as the troops were much in need of them. But the orders to proceed, without further delay, were imperative, and our successful return, at the close of five days, was expected.

The 14th, 20th and the greater part of the 15th corps, were left to attend well to the progressive siege of Savannah, and see to the military welfare of the Johnnies, and daily ascertain their manœuverings, and if necessary converse with them in true military style, until they either saw fit to take leg bail, or remain and pit themselves against the manly foe that were fast encircling them with its wiry folds, while the greater part of the 17th corps faithfully prosecuted the destruction of that strong arm of public road leading from the city to the Altamaha, thus severing it from all communications except by water.

I have previously noticed that the 2d brigade of our division was posted at the head of the Ogeechee canal, to prevent any molestation by cavalry inroads. In consequence, the 1st and 3d brigades only of our divison are along. After the preliminary duties of the morning were attended to, and all in proper readiness to depart, about 7 A. M., we pulled up stakes, and crossing the river on the bridge previously alluded to, we bade a temporary farewell to our remaining comrades, and pushed on our way. The country on the opposite side is very low and swampy, and principally used for the cultivation of rice—this being the only single outlet to the country beyond by means of the bridge—it was very badly cut up, and at spots almost impossible to traverse, it being at the time of which we are writing, completely blocked by the arrival and departure of trains. After groping in crowded columns for some hours through this narrow causeway, dodging in and out between the trains, we emerged into a more open space where we were more liberally supplied with elbow room. Our progress was at once accelerated, and we soon shortened the distance of our journey by rapid strides over the roads more favorable for easy transportation, and ere the setting of the sun, we had reached Midway Church, a dis-

tance of twenty miles or more, where we camped for the night, and throwing out
our pickets, details were made to go in quest of forage as hunger was pressing its
wants home to the keen susceptibilities of our nature, while others, as precautionary to a possible failure of its movement, started themselves on the track, and the
sensibilities of hunger, acted as a propelling power to urge them on the keen scented
trail.   Under its absolute want and necessity, it is often surprising to see the successful results with which their chase is rewarded, for, necessity often being the
mother of invention, their ingenious wits ferret out all needful supplies where you
would least look for its secretion.   However, as the hours of evening unconsciously
steal upon our senses, the timely arrival of sweet potatoes is made known, and the
welcome provision temporarily satisfies the calls of hunger and the pressing wants
of our frail natures.

One feature of interest presented itself here as worthy of notice, in the form of a
cemetry, whose ivy-decked walls, weeping willows, and moss covered trees, carried
one's thoughts to the memory of olden times, and forcibly reminded me of some of
those ancient and silent cities of the dead, that I had formerly witnessed in the old
world.   Its solemn and impressive scenery is well calculated to lead one to the
highest beatitude of contemplation, and bring up the most vivid reminiscences of
the past.   It was the burial place of some of those heroes of revolutionary celeb-
rity, and the receptacle of many a brave during the exciting times of 1812.   But
what a contrast now presents itself!   Could the spirit of those now solemnly resting beneath the classic shades of this most impressive spot, who had formerly con-
tended, manfully and heroically for the principles now sought to be trampled in the
dust, break the fetters of their prison house, and take a general view of the terrible realities of to-day, how would they blush and recoil with the most horrifying
intensity of feeling.   One would rather suppose that the exalted links of the past
as the monumental relics, presenting and portraying the sacrificed cost of so precious
a boon, would tend rather to arrest the uplifted hand of treason in its futile attempts
to destroy the darling of a mighty republic, and preserve its innocent memory for
the benefit of future generations.   Ye shades of Washington, Jefferson, Marion,
Patrick Henry and others, may your glorious deeds, your disinterested actions, your
love of freedom, and your purity of motive, rekindle anew in every member of
this broad republic the fires of liberty, until the heart of every sire and son shall
burn with holy indignation against the vain attempts of those who seek its assassin-
ation ; and may its fruits and blessings be emblazoned and enstamped upon univer-
sal nature, and rock and rill, glen and dale reverberate with its mighty chorus, and
roll the swell of its musical symphonies through all the earth.   The next day witnessed our early preparation to resume still further our journey in order to the full
accomplishment of what we had in view.

The night had been sultry and close for the season of the year, and the heavy
dews peculiar to this climate, during the silent hours, cames drizzling down like
misty rain, completely saturating our blankets and everything else that would yield
to its subtle influence.   Taking an early start, about noon we reached the town of
Walthourville, most of its wealthy inhabitants having fled previous to our arrival,
leaving us in undisputed possession of its narrow defined limits.   It contained a
court house, a few churches, and some very neat and tasty dwellings.   It is the
county seat of Liberty County, and had more the air of an aristocratic resort, than
that of business.   Like most Southern towns, its population could not have been

very dense, as it was too wide spread for the number of dwellings to admit of such. But before our army emerged from its centre to continue its further advance, the interior of many of its mansions must have presented a revolutionary appearance, judging from the number of articles to be seen in the possession of those favoring them with a visit. And could many of the fair damsels have heard and seen the jokes and amusements that were enjoyed at their expense in the perusal of their former correspondence, much of which partook of the extreme of secrecy, it would have created the rosy blush and painted the fair cheek with a crimson hue that would have told its own tale, and no doubt would have developed a firm resolve to prepare better for its safe keeping in their future experience; and for the benefit of those who have entertained the thought that the fair sex would never condescend and yield to union pressure in the firm endeavor to preserve a once glorious union, I have the pleasure of informing such, that much of the correspondence referred to already, entirely conflicted with such notions, and rather breathed a disposition already prepared, to return to their former allegiance at the presentation of a favorable opportunity for the same. But whether the evidence of a general upheaving and overturning of their once happy homes, will change the general tenor of their sentiments and feelings or not, I am not prepared to state.

Some of the negro population, whose heads were white with age, and whose forms were fast yielding to the inevitable pressure of time, seemed overjoyed at the introduction of so many Yanks, and were completely surprised to see such a fine looking set of fellows, as we evidently appeared to them, to be transferred from the descriptive Yankees of their masters that was to have answered and characterized our appearance among them. They were thoroughly disarmed of all dread, prejudice and fear, and clapped their hands and exhibited their ivory as though they were in a perfect ecstacy of delight, and gave active demonstrations of satisfaction, by trying the flexibility of their limbs, now stiffened with age,—dancing from the promptings of the heart instead of the head. Their motions were not such as would have suited a Broadway audience, nor calculated to electrify the gay pleasure seekers of the 19th century, but answered well their style and manner of conveying their supreme delight and unbounded satisfaction, at our short but decisive visit. Leaving the town, we made good our advance, as it was necessary to establish our camping quarters near the terminus of our intended trip, to prepare for the enforcement of railroad law on the morrow. During the afternoon we passed some bad places, but the weather being favorable for the preservation of the roads in good order, and having no trains to accompany us, we measured our pace pretty rapidly, and "leaving those things that are behind, we pressed forward to those that are before," and eventually brought up in camp about 5½ P. M., some 57 miles from the city and about six miles from the Altamaha river. The country being level, the roads are all of artificial construction, and the water principally used by us, is from adjoining swamps, as springs here are entirely out of the question. Sweet potatoes being the only article of diet, the preparation for supper does not consume much time, and during the course of the evening, the boys can be seen in true paddy style collecting around their kettles helping themselves to this production of negro labor, doing ample justice to those yellow esculents of the coast.

The day being warm and the distance traveled pretty considerable, the boys that "played out" during the day, are, during the hours of evening, wending their way to their respective regiments, feeling somewhat worsted by the day's march, and being behind time in the preparation of their evening meal, do not feel in the best of humor at this style of military treatment, but before morning all is plunged in the land of forgetfulness, and a new start is taken for future action. In due time on the morning of the 19th, the two brigades pulled out for the railroad, about three-fourths of a mile to our right. The 1st brigade going toward the river and destroying the same back toward camp, while the 3d brigade went below some three miles, both meeting at night in near proximity to the camp. While the cavalry (Kilpatrick's) protected the front and flanks. During the day our brigades succeeded in the thorough destruction of some six miles of its length and within two or three miles of the railroad bridge that spans the river at this point of the Atlantic and Gulf Railroad. All was accomplished and passed off with unusual good success, returning to camp shortly before dusk. The third and fourth divisions tearing up and destroying the same below and between us and the city. At an early hour of the following day, not hearing punctually from the cavalry at the front, we pulled out in the direction of the river, the advance regiment going about four miles from camp, and within two of the bridge, and gaining the desired information, we about faced and started on the backward track. Our intention was, if possible, to destroy the river bridge, if it could be accomplished without too great a sacrifice of life. But finding the bridge strongly fortified and defended, and its approach difficult of access, the prospect of its destruction was abandoned, and both cavalry and infantry could be seen rapidly gliding over the track by which we came. The chances and prospects of securing forage on the return route would be very slim and scant, and in consequence it became a necessity for us to make good our speed, and accelerate our progress as fast as circumstances would possibly admit, and could we have been reviewed that day, the reviewing officer would have been necessitated to have made good use of the organs of sight, to have detected any deficiencies in our exterior appearance. To say we marched is not strictly truthful; in fact, we flew over the road as only a soldier can when empty haversacks stare them in the face and hard tack is promised on our reaching a certain defined goal or temporary depot of supplies. We had been informed that on reaching Midway Church, we would make good the same, and long ere darkness set in, we reached the zenith of our success, having traveled over 30 miles during the day on the strength of a few potatoes: and if it is necessary for "Sherman's raiders or bummers," as we are sometimes styled, to take a strong fort or breastwork—let the Johnnies exhibit a few boxes of hard tack, and I will venture for its successful capture and possession. For in raiding life, hard bread is a rarity, as I have often seen as high as from one to five dollars paid for a few of those dainty specimens of the staff of life, and sometimes almost incredible sums paid for dainty productions of the table by those whose palates are very sensitive to delicate morsels. It is not true that the soldiers lose their relish for the delicacies of civilized life, but rather the contrary, for in proportion to the depressed condition of our sanitary supplies, and its inferior quality, the appetite of the soldier boys become more keenly whetted for the voracious destruction of the palatable contents of a well supplied larder, and as they think of home and its former comforts and the rich repasts they formerly enjoyed, they almost fancy themselves on the borders of the land of plenty, and in scenting distance of the headquarters of some very tasty pastry cook, but those flitting fanciful visions soon disappear, leaving its unfortunate victim to find that he is only in the shadowy realms of dreamland, the dupe of these flitting spectres that often deceive the senses, and lead us through the mysterious labyrinths of delusion, and find eventually that we are still only at the starting point of our etherial or aerial flight. It is often surprising after such severe marching as the past twelve hours, to find the boys ever ready for the various freaks manifested after reaching camp. The negro boys scattered in the several companies of the regiment, generally prove an unfailing source of affording much pastime and enjoyment; for it is no uncommon occurrence to see large groups of the boys form a large circle, with negro performers hemmed in the centre, performing their comic movements, and going through their dancing jigs with quite an air of satisfaction, while one of their number, to supply the want of music, in constant and correct measure, is repeating a ditty in some such language as the following—

"As my sweetheart goes round and round,
The hollow of her foot makes a hole in the ground."

Some of them having become perfect adepts in the business from long practice, and considering the untoward circumstances of their training, would surprise many by their agility of movement and promptitude of action in strict accordance with time. Late in the evening a supply of "Uncle Sam's" hard tack arrived, and although many had turned in for the night and yielded their senses to the softly stealing slumbers of repose, its arrival simply required a bare announcement ere they could be seen evacuating their nests in order to secure their apportionment of the welcome supplies. This is the first issued to us now for the space of fourteen days, and to a civilian the most sumptuous table would not appear more inviting than did this important article of army diet to the table. Why, they devoured them as though they were creamed and sugared over! and were welcomed as the most precious boon of life. Talk of feasts! This was a "feast of fat things," not of "wines on the lees well refined," but hard tack well suited to a hungry stomach, prepared for its reception. After attending to a proper disposition of our share, it being late, we turned in for the night, to be better prepared for the morrow's task, with a light heart at the timely arrival of our old visitor. To troops in garrison, hard bread may be but poor living, but to troops in the field it ever proves a "friend in need," as well as a "friend indeed."

On the morning of the 21st, long'ere the break of day, we are again on the road for our old camp. At half past three, A. M., our slumbers were abruptly terminated, and at five A. M., we could be seen in line of march under full sail, with the intention of reaching our destination ere night enveloped us with her sombre curtain. The previous night had been showery, and the bracing air of the morning was favorable to our rapid progress, and it may well be judged that we spared no pains to improve the opportunity. But as nature in her various garbs and freaks, does not see fit to consult our taste, when about to change her appearance and treatment, before we had traveled many miles, opened the portals of her atmospheric storehouse, and amused herself by pouring down through her drenching sieve the watery element in such profusion as completely to saturate our persons and clothes. And the departing as well as returning forage trains, in connection with bad roads, so thoroughly blocked the way as materially to hinder our progress. But about half past four, P. M., we again crossed the Ogeechee river, but without as much as a salutary halt near the river, we make good our exit for a timely arrival to pay our usual respects and customary salute to our old place of sojourn. And soon after dark we were permitted to see the old place left five days since. The evening was intensely cold and wood and water being very scarce, it was not as welcome a friend as it would have been under more favorable auspices. Thus in the short space of five days we marched the distance of 120 miles, and spent one day of the time in the destruction of six miles of railroad on the strength of a scanty supply of sweet potatoes, and together with the other division had secured the destruction of that strip of the Atlanta and Gulf Railroad leading from Savannah to the Altamaha river, leaving the city to the enjoyment of water communications only, as every railroad that verged to its centre is now cut off—leaving her to trust principally to the patronage and use of Neptune's highway until the dawn of peace shall lead to the successful reconstruction of those important highways of modern civilization, now in ruins as the fruit of treason's hand of self destruction.

While we were engaged in the task of which we have written, the remainder of our army was busily engaged in the vigorous prosecution of the siege until the night of the 20th, when the rebel troops evcuated the city, and respectfully withdrew to another strategical point of operations, and early on the evening of the 21st our forces triumphantly entered the city, the 20th corps entering first, and subsequently garrisoned the same, and during the few days following, our whole army established their camps at a respectable distance from its precincts, our division taking up its position near Fort Thunderbolt, south of the city. At the rebel abandonment everything was left in a good state of preservation, and pretty much all the light and heavy ordnance left in our possession, together with a large amount of stores and 30,000 bales of cotton. Large numbers of the rebel army secreted themselves, and subsequently gave themselves up to our disposal. Some garbed themselves in female attire to secure their liberty from a service and cause they considered hopeless. In short, everything pretty much was left in our possession, and our success was grand, final and complete.

CHAPTER VII.

A GENERAL RECAPITULATION OF OPERATIONS IN GEORGIA.

Army in the Spring—Fall of Dalton and Resaca—Operations at Dallas—Operations near the Big Kenesaw—The Siege—The Stars and Stripes on its Lofty Summit—Unburied Dead—Operations at Nickajack Creek—Move to the Right—Move to the Left—Terrible Conflict of July 22d—Move to the Extreme Right—The Battle of the 28th—Vigorous Prosecution of the Siege—Final Flank Movement—Rebel Army Cut in Two—Evacuation of the City—Slocum's Entrance—Everything left in our Possession—Close of the Campaign—Chase after Hood—Thomas left in Charge—Return to Marietta—Closing Remarks.

Thus during the brief space of three months, that brave army that lay nestling in the lap of spring, had accomplished an almost incredible succession of brilliant achievements, and secured a firm lodgment on the coast. During the latter part of April and the first of May, this powerful army of the service having enjoyed partial rest and repose during the winter months, in preparation for the season's contest, began to develop their energies anew; and from the several railroads leading from Nashville, Knoxville, and other places centering in Chattanooga, they could be seen rapidly concentrating and massing together in effective force—the whole converging near the field of contest, and taking their proper places on the different parts of the line assigned them by their commanders; not the raw recruits of three years since, but a well disciplined army, having previously well tested their energy and skill in constant contact with the foe at every strategical point of their own selection. The almost impregnable line of position from Tunnel Hill and Dalton to Resaca were the first points to be assaulted; and although they bade defiance to us in their strong natural and artificial intrenchments, yet, about the middle of May we compelled them, under cover of the night, to betake themselves to flight; and so close and rapid did we pursue them that they could not successfully accomplish the burning of the railroad bridge that lay near the town, and killed and wounded a large number of them on their retreat, the dead, wounded and dying being left in our hands for care, as they had no time to secure their possession. Falling back to Alatoona Pass, Lost Mountain, and the rugged bluffs in the vicinity of Dallas, Paulding County, we closely pursued them thither, the Army of the Tennessee occupying the extreme right at Resaca, under McPherson. It is again selected for that position at Dallas, at which place we arrived early on the morning of the 27th, and at once butted against the foe in-waiting. At this important point we experienced some stubborn fighting, and met the oft repeated assaults of the enemy in their persistent endeavor to dislodge us and make a breach in our lines. After several days steady fighting at this very difficult position, we gradually, in the best of order, fell back to the vicinity of Acworth, when, resting a couple of days, we pushed forward to near Big Shanty. On the plains that lay sleeping near the rugged heights of the Kenesaw Mountains we next engaged them. After several days of heavy skirmishing, daily narrowing our lines as we stealthily advanced, under cover of the night, we secured a firm foothold at its base. Having compelled their evacuation of one of the strongest artificial line of works witnessed during the campaign, and their approach defended by a strong abatis of brush and trees, together with lines of driven spikes and timber felled in every direction. Then commenced what may be considered the siege proper of the Towering Kenesaw, which lasted about two weeks. In the interim there was constant stubborn fighting on some part of the lines, on both sides, and incessant skirmishing every day. During the night of July 2d and early on the morning of the 3d, the rebels evacuated their well selected position, and left our army victors of the spot. At early day, the color bearer of our regiment was the first to plant the stars and stripes on its lofty summit, and unfold the banner to the breeze, and ere the sun was reflected in the horizon, its graceful folds could be seen floating proudly on the mountain top, from which the stars and bars had been previously ejected. Some of the unburied dead of our regiment that we could not inter on that memorable day of June 27th, were shortly after buried beneath the sod that covered its slopeing sides, saturated with the last ebbing tide of life's crimson blood that flowed from many a reeking victim to the cause of justice and liberty. We next pursued them to Nickajack Creek, where we had sharp fighting on July 4th, and extended our lines the few following days, as far to the right as Howell's Ford, on the Chattahoochie river. After the settlement of matters at this point, on the morning of the 9th, we started for the extreme left by way of Marietta to the Rosswell factories on the margin of the Chattaoochie, crossing the river on the morning of the 11th ; the distance travelled was thirty miles. The factories and bridges that spanned the river had been previously burned by the cavalry, but we effected a crossing over a temporary foot bridge erected for the purpose. During the day we threw up a line of works, and remained in position, to rest our exhausted frames, and recruit strength for future action. On the morning of the 17th we pulled up stakes and circled around still more to the left, bringing up at Decatur, on the line of road from Atlanta to Augusta, and about six miles from the city, while another part of our forces was engaged in destroying the railroad as far out as Stone Mountain. Having reached about within shelling distance of the "Gate City," the point of our attention and the goal of our campaign, we knocked for admittance to its centre, and politely demanded its surrender to our victorious arms, but was stubbornly refused. Then commenced a thorough investment of its limit. We so surprised them at our sudden appearance at Decatur, as to prevent the escape of a long train of cars bound for Augusta, together with a lot of other stuff, all of which they set fire to in their hurried flight. They inflicted a slight damage on us before we felt their whereabouts, but we soon erected a strong semi-circle of earthworks and forts. July 22d, the rebel commander, Gen. Hood, massed the greatest bulk of his command to bear on our extreme left, with the intention if possible, to completely turn our flank, and with irresistible fury to roll back the advancing tide of our arms that were fast completing a circle, dangerous to their existance in the city; but the Army of the Tennessee met nobly the mighty shock so impulsive and terrible at the first onslaught, and although we did not turn the intended defeat into a flush of victory, yet we so thwarted the wily foe in the consummation of their plans, that they were anxious to hastily retire in utter disgust of their complete failure. The fight commenced shortly before mid-day, and lasted about four hours, and in that short space of time, the slaughter was terrible and the number of the dead and dying was appalling. But at the close of the conflict, we were masters still of the ground we occupied previous to the contest.

In the early part of this struggle we lost a brave commander in the person of Maj. Gen. J. B. McPherson. I had the honor of being by his side during his last dying moments. The only expression escaping his lips, being a request for his hat which was not near him, and which with his sword, I could not find—they having been previously taken by some one. I was present when the rebels took his papers and marine glass, &c., but they committed no further depredations on his person. Those articles were subsequently re-captured during the engagement by members of the company to which I belong, and turned over to division head-quarters. But a variety of other articles were secured by Geo. Reynolds of Co. D, 15th Iowa Infantry and myself, and turned over to Lt. Col. Strong of staff; and although I have been entirely wronged of the credit due me for repeated exertions and exposure in the endeavor to secure the body from (what was at the time) the rebel vantage ground, under a galling artillery fire, and the constant appearance of rebel stragglers lurking in the immediate vicinity where he lay; yet I am contented with the satisfaction that I performed my duty, and only wish that I could have done more under the deeply tragic circumstances of his death. Strongly fortifying our position, on the night of the 26th and day of the 27th, we stealthily pulled out and circled around to the extreme right, where we at once felt their whereabouts, and found them waiting to give us a warm reception. About noon of the 28th, commenced another bloody conflict, the rebel commander having risked another flanking speculation, in the endeavor to accomplish on the right what he utterly failed to do on the left. It was for some time with us "nip and tuck." In fact we felt we had more than we bargained for, but eventually arrested their onslaught and held them in check, and inflicted upon them a most terrible blow, giving them to understand that turning Sherman's flanks, was a problem not so easily solved, and a task not easy to accomplish. The rebel loss in this engagement was fearful, as on parts of the field they literally lay piled one upon another, while ours was remarkably light in consideration of the heavy and constant firing that characterized the time of the engagement. During the ensuing four weeks, we gave them all they could possibly do to maintain their position in their works without openly attacking us. Skirmishing heavy day and night with them, we steadily advanced our lines until we had completed three strong lines of breastworks and forts.

During the nights of August 25th and 26th, we managed to steal quietly away from the siege, and proceeded on our last flank movement which resulted in the capture of the city. Marching to the West Point and Montgomery railroad, we completely destroyed some 15 miles of the same, and filled up some of the deep cuts, thus effectually preventing their use of that end of the road. This being done on the morning of the 30th, we started for the only line of railroad communication left them, and brought up in the vicinity of Jonesboro on the evening of the same day. During the 30th of August and 1st of September, there was some terrible heavy fighting on both sides, which resulted in our possession of the railroad, and the severing of their army in twain. After gaining possession of the railroad, the rebels immediately evacuated the city, previously blowing up their arsenals and magazines, and destroying thirty car loads of ammunition, leaving all their heavy ordnance and a large amount of other stuff in our possession. Gen. Slocum's command was the first to enter the city, as their position was near it. We followed the rebels some distance down to get them well on the retreat, and then commenced a retrograde course—arriving in camp with the remainder of the army near East Point about noon of September 8th, having completed the object of the campaign and secured a firm occupation and foothold in the heart and centre of the Confederacy.

Having finished the campaign, it was intended the army should enjoy a short respite from active service, but ere we had fairly looked around, our rest was disturbed by Hood getting in our rear and destroying the only line of our supplies. Making a feint on the West Point and Montgomery railroad, preparatory to pursuit, Thomas' command, and the Army of Tennessee started in hot haste after the dashing rebel leader, going over much of the ground fought and contested for during the summer. We caught up with him near Snake's Gap, and compelling him from the line of railroad, and Thomas getting in his rear, Sherman left him in charge of the rebel forces, to watch and keep track of them, while he, with the remainder of his army, circled down the Blue Mountains, somewhat prolonging our stay, by almost entirely living off the country. In our return trip from the pursuit of Hood, we cleared the country of almost everything in the shape of eatables, &c., and entirely disabled it from actively participating in the future strife of the rebellion, taking the precaution to destroy all the bridges that spanned the streams in our course, relieved the prospect and chances of cavalry dashes along the line of railroad between Chattanooga and Kingston, and prevented the rapid progress of the enemy, should he see fit to about face and start in pursuit of our forces. Everything valuable that was easy of removal was taken from Rome to Chattanooga, and public works destroyed, thus rendering that city of no avail for the future uses of treason. Resting a few days near Galeville, situated on the margin of the Chattooga river, on the morning of the 20th of October we left that part of the field, and started for Ruff's Station, passing, in our route, Cedar Bluffs, Cave Springs, Cedar Town, Dallas, Slateville, Van Wirt, and the Lost Mountains, respectively establishing camp at Ruff's Station, a few miles below Marietta, on the evening of November 5th. Everything in the pathway of Sherman's terrible army was made to feel keenly the scourge of war as ne'er they felt before, and only a few chimney stacks (Sherman's unmistakable monuments) was left to witness that any of those previously named towns ever had an existence. While our army was engaged in this roundabout trip, the construction corps was busily engaged in repairing the damage done to the railroad; and that being completed, the previously accumulated supplies at Chattanooga was rapidly conveyed to Atlanta in sufficient quantity to load the army trains in preparation for our march to the sea. This being done, all the sick and convalescents were sent back, and the troops scattered along the line of railroad hurriedly collected for the ensuing campaign. On the 9th and 10th of November the troops received eight months pay, and everything being in readiness to depart, on the 12th we snapped our only link of communication with the North, and started on our race for a view of Neptune's watery dominions, leaving our loyal supporters in the North to guess our destination, and while they were wrapt in the coiling labyrinth of mysticism as to our daily progress, we were busily engaged searching the most secret nooks of the Confederate center, and making another grand rend through their anarchical dominions. While the important undertaking was considered by many in the North a rash one, and Europe was hourly expecting to hear of our disgraceful defeat and a demoralizing flight, Sherman, with the irresistible advance of his army, was making rapid and gigantic strides toward the coast, sounding, to the very quick, the metal of the Confederacy, and plainly demonstrated its internal deficiency and weakness, and proved its inability to long maintain a successful warfare against a combined North. The high sounding vaunts and pretensions of the South in its early claims to chivalry, and their boasted ability to establish self-government despite the combined efforts of the North, with all their fanciful and glorious dreams of a mighty republic—based on slavery as the corner stone—was entirely exploded by the successful accomplishment of the undertaking. and all Europe taken by the ears at the startling developments that resulted.

Up to the capture and occupation of Savannah from the first, the army of the Tennessee had travelled in marches and counter marches, movements and counter movements, and in flanking operations, some 1,650 miles. Five months of the time was spent under the constant booming of cannon, and the cracking of musketry. Over one hundred days of the time was spent in hand to hand skirmishing with the enemy day and night, and weeks of the time was spent in the water-soaked trenches, with nothing but the canopy of heaven for our shelter. We fought a number of battles such as Resaca, Dallas, Kenesaw, Nickajack Creek, Chattaoochie River, and Decatur, Georgia. In the Atlanta siege, July 22 & 28, on the left and right flanks respectively, Jonesboro, and a number of minor engagements at different times—took two strongly fortified cities, several well fortified towns, and a number of strong natural positions, such as Snake's Gap, Dallas, Alatoona Pass, Lost and Kenesaw mountains, and the Chattahoochie river ; the most important flank movements, such as Resaca, Dallas, Howell's Ford, on the Chattahoochie, Rossewell Factories on the same river, Decatur to the Stone Mountain, and to the right flank on July 27th and 28th, and Jonesboro. Also from the siege of Savannah to Fort McAllister and the Altamaha river—in all of which we were successful.

Our whole army wrested from the rebels nearly 500 miles length of territory— burnt several hundred miles of railroad—severed the Confederacy in thrice—took several thousand prisoners, extensive quantities of ordnance and other stores of every description—captured some 50,000 bales of cotton for the Government— destroyed much more in our campaign through the State—despoiled them of several arsenals and foundries for the manufacture of light and heavy ordnance; and during the time we did not call on Uncle Sam for over an average of one half rations, taking the remainder from the enemy. We succeeded completely in demoralizing and scattering their western armies, thus rendering them weak and ineffective. Took possession of Georgia's proud capital, and humbled its once exultant and defiant rulers. In fact it may be strictly claimed, that we conquered the State. Not to rule with an iron rod, but for the suppression of anarchy and civil strife. Our losses were heavy during the Atlanta campaign, but they were equally as heavy on the part of the enemy. Thus have we demonstrated to the north, as well as the world, the possible and successful penetration of an enemy's country through its interior; and if Napoleon failed in the successful penetration of Russia's centre, Sherman has succeeded beyond all expectation in spanning the proud dominions of the rebellious South. While the North was locked in the icy barriers of winter, and Lieut. Gen. Grant was fast tightening the cords that was to sever the head of rebellion—Sherman, with his powerful army was disemboweling the rebellious interior, and severing its main arterial channels of circulating life—thus cutting short the career of its existence, and rapidly reducing it to a skeleton form, as at the present time I write, its breathing apparatus has ceased its vibrations, and its principal leaders are awaiting the trial and punishment of their enormous crime. To accomplish this, the troops have experienced untold sufferings, in the constant daily exposure to every conceivable hardship. Not only have they repeatedly braved the fury of the storm and tempest of terrible battle, but they have, during the inclemency of the winter season, daily waded the almost interminable and impenetrable swamps of the Carolinas. For the space of two months they were scarcely a day without wet feet, and much of the time barefoot and the whole person ragged—seldom enjoying the privilege of a salutary change of clothing, for want of soap and other articles absolutely necessary. For the suppression of this rebellion, and the partial restoration of law and order, they have in addition to all other hardships consequent on our arrival in the vicinity of Washington, marched in an aggregate over 3,000 miles of territory, according to the daily account of the same ; and although they have gone for months without pay, mail and a number of other privileges. Yet no army ever put up with the same inconveniences, with less complaint. With true devotion to their leader, they with alacrity have always gone where he in duty called them, but although the task required, has sometimes proved difficult of accomplishment, and the treatment appeared rather harsh, yet their invariable conclusion was, "He did it all for the best." No army commander ever better won the good will and opinion of his troops than Sherman, as he is almost idolized by them. And the nation ought to be truly thankful that such men as Generals Grant, Sherman and others have been raised up, whose sole purpose and aim has been to speedily terminate the struggle, and prostrate the rebellious elements that characterize the modern state of things.

I cannot close this brief sketch without acknowledging that, whilst our army has done much, even more than reasonably could have been expected from them, and have entitled themselves to the highest respect and lasting gratitude of the nation —yet that above all, our most especial attention should be directed to the Ruler of Nations, whose mysterious "hand writing" can be distinctly traced in lines of blood, through this terrible crucible of affliction of the past four years, and although He has sometimes suspended the drapery of blackest night over the horizon of our National existence ; yet, with His gentle hand of mercy, He has withdrawn the threatening cloud and exhibited the infinite wisdom that led to its timely display. And in this grand succession of storm and calm, the heightening and dissolving views of an All-wise providence, have been beautifully reflected in our National atmosphere.